America FAQ

Coen Nishiumi

Level 5

IBC パブリッシング

はじめに

　ラダーシリーズは、「はしご (ladder)」を使って一歩一歩上を目指すように、学習者の実力に合わせ、無理なくステップアップできるよう開発された英文リーダーのシリーズです。

　リーディング力をつけるためには、繰り返したくさん読むこと、いわゆる「多読」がもっとも効果的な学習法であると言われています。多読では、「1. 速く 2. 訳さず英語のまま 3. なるべく辞書を使わず」に読むことが大切です。スピードを計るなど、速く読むよう心がけましょう（たとえば TOEIC® テストの音声スピードはおよそ 1 分間に 150 語です）。そして 1 語ずつ訳すのではなく、英語を英語のまま理解するくせをつけるようにします。こうして読み続けるうちに語感がついてきて、だんだんと英語が理解できるようになるのです。まずは、ラダーシリーズの中からあなたのレベルに合った本を選び、少しずつ英文に慣れ親しんでください。たくさんの本を手にとるうちに、英文書がすらすら読めるようになってくるはずです。

《本シリーズの特徴》
- 中学校レベルから中級者レベルまで5段階に分かれています。自分に合ったレベルからスタートしてください。
- クラシックから現代文学、ノンフィクション、ビジネスと幅広いジャンルを扱っています。あなたの興味に合わせてタイトルを選べます。
- 巻末のワードリストで、いつでもどこでも単語の意味を確認できます。レベル1、2では、文中の全ての単語が、レベル3以上は中学校レベル外の単語が掲載されています。
- カバーにヘッドホーンマークのついているタイトルは、オーディオ・サポートがあります。ウェブから購入／ダウンロードし、リスニング教材としても併用できます。

《使用語彙について》
レベル1：中学校で学習する単語約1000語
レベル2：レベル1の単語＋使用頻度の高い単語約300語
レベル3：レベル1の単語＋使用頻度の高い単語約600語
レベル4：レベル1の単語＋使用頻度の高い単語約1000語
レベル5：語彙制限なし

CONTENTS

Chapter 1
The Land of the United States of America and Its People アメリカの大地と人...1

USA Territory アメリカの国土 2

Q: How large is the USA? 2
国土の広さは？

Q: When did USA territory gain its present form? 3
領土はいつ決まったの？

Q: What are the areas, besides the 48 contiguous states, that compose the USA? 4
本土以外にも領土はあるの？

Geographical and Natural Features of the USA アメリカの地形と自然 4

Q: What are the USA's natural features? 4
自然の特徴は？

Q: What kind of mountain ranges does the USA have? 5
どんな山や山脈があるの？

Q: What kind of lakes are the Great Lakes? 6
五大湖とは？

Q: What kind of river is the Mississippi? 7
ミシシッピ川とは？

Q: What kind of national parks does the USA have? 8
どんな国立公園があるの？

The Climate of the USA アメリカの気候 9

Q: What are the characteristics of the American climate? 9
気候の特徴は？

Q: Do tornadoes really occur in various places? 10
竜巻はどこで起きるの？

Q: Does the USA have earthquakes like Japan? 11
地震はあるの？

Q: How is a hurricane different from a typhoon? 11
ハリケーンは台風と違う？

The People of America アメリカ人 12

Q: How has the American population changed? 12
人口の推移は？

Q: What kinds of people emigrated to the USA from Europe? 13
ヨーロッパからの移民とは？

Q: What phenomenon does the term "Asian Power" refer to? 14
アジア系パワーとは？

Q: What is the current ethnic make-up of the USA population? 15
どんな民族がいるの？

Q: What kind of people make up the white population in America? 17
白人とはどういう人たち？

Q: Who does the word "WASP" refer to? 18
ワスプとはどのような人？

Q: What kind of influence have people from Latin countries had in the USA? 18
ラテン系の人々の影響とは？

Q: Which people does the word "blacks" refer to? 19
黒人とはどのような人たち？

Q: What is the social status of blacks in the USA? 20
黒人系の人々のアメリカでの地位は？

Q: What is the real meaning of "Jewish Power"? 21
ユダヤ系のパワーとは？

Q: Why are Indians called Native Americans? 23
ネイティブ・アメリカンとは？

Q: How have relations between Native Americans and other Americans changed? 24
ネイティブ・アメリカンの人口は？

Q: What influences did Americans receive from Native Americans? 25
ネイティブ・アメリカンの影響とは？

Q: What does the word "diversity" mean? 25
多様性の意味は？

Q: Is English the national language in the USA? 26
英語は国語か？

The Differences in Regions in the USA アメリカの地域性 27

Q: What kind of region is New England? 27
ニューイングランドはどんな所？

Q: Do New York and Los Angeles represent East and West Coast cultures? 28
東西の文化を代表する都市は？

Q: What is the Midwest, or the "Heartland," like as a region? 30
ハートランド、ミッドウエストはどんな所？

Q: What kind of region is the South? 31
サウスはどんな所？

Chapter 2
History and Background of the USA アメリカの歴史と背景 33

National Anthem and Flag アメリカの国家と国旗 34

Q: What is the national anthem of the USA? 34
アメリカ国歌とは？

Q: What is the history of the design of American flag? 35
アメリカ国旗とは？

The History of the USA アメリカの歴史 36

Q: How old is America? 36
アメリカが独立国になったのはいつ？

Q: What was America like before Independence? 37
独立する前のアメリカの状況は？

Q: How did America decide to become independent? 38
どのようにして独立したの？

Q: What were the various stages in the War of Independence (The American Revolution)? 39
独立戦争とは？

Q: What situation did America find itself in after independence? 40
独立後のアメリカは？

Q: When did westward development start in America? .. 41
西部開拓が始まったのはいつ？

Q: When was Texas incorporated into the USA? 42
テキサス州はいつアメリカになったの？

Q: What was the Oregon Trail? 43
オレゴン・トレイルとは？

Q: What was the Civil War about? 44
南北戦争とは？

Q: When did development start in California? 46
いつ頃カリフォルニアは発展したのか？

Q: Why has America shown so much growth in the twentieth century? 47
20世紀にアメリカが発展した理由は？

Q: What did WWI mean for the USA? 48
アメリカにとっての第一次世界大戦とは？

Q: What led the USA to join WWII? 49
アメリカが第二次世界大戦に突入した理由は？

Q: What impact did the Vietnam War have on the USA? . 50
ベトナム戦争の影響とは？

USA Public Opinion and the American Disposition アメリカの世論、アメリカ人気質 51

Q: Who were the most popular presidents in America? .. 51
最も人気のある大統領は？

Q: How has the Americans' view of the Japanese changed? 52
アメリカ人の日本観は？

Q: What is the most important American value? 54
アメリカ人が大切にする価値観とは？

Chapter 3
American Politics アメリカの政治 55

American Democracy アメリカの民主主義 56

Q: What is the relationship between state and federal governments? 56
連邦政府と地方政府の関係は？

Q: What is the history behind the Democratic and Republican Parties? 57
民主党と共和党の違いとは？

Q: How does the electoral system work? 59
選挙システムは？

Q: What is the role of the president of the United States of America? 60
アメリカ大統領の役割は？

Q: What are the roles of the US president and Congress, and how are they related? 61
大統領と議会の役割は？

Q: What do people think of the Bush Administration? 62
ブッシュ政権の評価？

Q: What brought about the election of Barack Obama? 63
バラク・オバマが大統領になった経緯は？

The Judicial System and Human Rights アメリカの法体系と人権 64

Q: What are the characteristics of the US Constitution? 64
合衆国憲法の特徴は？

Q: What are "civil rights"?..66
公民権とは？

Q: What do Americans do to counteract prejudice and discrimination?..67
偏見や差別に対する活動はあるの？

Q: What are the characteristics of the US trial system?..69
裁判制度の特徴は？

Q: What is legal bargaining in the USA? 70
司法取引とは？

Q: Is there capital punishment in the USA? 70
死刑制度はあるの？

Domestic Affairs アメリカの内政 71

Q: What is the size, total revenue, and expenditure of the current US federal budget? 71
国家予算の規模と収支は？

Q: What kind of police system exists in the USA? 72
警察制度の特徴とは？

Q: What are the characteristics of the American tax system?..73
税制の特徴とは？

Q: How does the US educational system differ from the Japanese system?..74
教育制度の特徴とは？

Welfare and Health アメリカの福祉と健康 75

Q: What is the major cause of death among Americans?..75
アメリカで多い死因は？

Q: What kind of health insurance system does the USA have? 76
健康保険制度の特徴は？

American Diplomacy アメリカの外交......................77

Q: What is US isolationism? 77
アメリカの孤立主義とは？

Q: In what ways did US diplomacy change after the end of the Cold War? 78
冷戦後のアメリカ外交は？

Q: What is "human rights diplomacy"? 79
人権外交とはどのような外交？

Q: What is the relationship of the USA with the UN? 80
アメリカと国連の関係は？

Q: How has US diplomacy with Japan changed? 81
対日外交の推移は？

Q: What effect did 9/11 have on America? 82
アメリカにとっての9.11は？

Q: How do people feel about the assassination of Osama Bin Laden? 84
オサマ・ビン・ラディンをどう思うか？

American Military and Space Development アメリカの軍事と宇宙開発 86

Q: Does the USA still place an emphasis on the military? .. 86
アメリカの軍事力は？

Q: How is the CIA thought of in the USA? 87
CIAの評価は？

Q: What is the future of US space development? 88
宇宙開発の将来は？

Chapter 4
The US Economy アメリカの経済活動 89

Background of the US Economy アメリカ経済の背景 ... 90

Q: What kind of currency is the US dollar? 90
アメリカの通貨は？

Q: When did the US dollar begin to have international distribution? 91
ドルが基軸通貨になったのはいつ？

Q: What regional differences exist in the US domestic economy? 92
国内の経済活動の特徴は？

Q: What shifts have there been in the US trade balance? . 92
貿易収支の推移は？

Q: What items does the US export and import? 93
何を輸出・輸入しているの？

Q: What is the Lehman Shock? 94
リーマンショックとは？

Q: What will the future of environment-related businesses be? 95
環境関連ビジネスの将来は？

US Industries アメリカの産業界 96

Q: What is the current situation of the US auto industry? .. 96
自動車業界の現状は？

Q: What is the current state of the US computer industry? 97
コンピュータ産業の現状は？

Q: What kind of place is Silicon Valley? 98
シリコンバレーとはどんなところ？

Q: What future trends can be foreseen in the US space industry? 99
今後の宇宙産業？

Q: What is the current state of US agriculture? 100
農業の現状は？

Q: What is the current state of America's IT industry? 101
IT産業の現状は？

American Management and Office Environments アメリカの経営と職場環境 102

Q: What does sexual harassment refer to in the USA? .. 102
社内でのセクハラとは？

Q: What is equal opportunity in corporate management? 103
企業経営でのイコーリティとは？

Q: What are American working hours? 104
労働時間は長い、短い？

Q: What is the wage standard in the US? 105
賃金水準は高い、低い？

Q: What are some characteristics of the way Americans run businesses? 105
アメリカ式経営の特徴は？

Chapter 5
Society—Life 社会・生活 107

The American Living Environment
アメリカの生活環境 108

Q: What is the relationship between upper-middle class and low-income families? 108
社会階層はあるの？

Q: Do gay people receive equal treatment in the US? ... 109
同性愛者はどう扱われている？

Q: Which cities and areas in the US are the most popular? 110
人気のある都市や地域はどこ？

Religion 宗教 111

Q: What are the characteristics of religion in the USA? 111
アメリカの宗教の特徴は？

Q: What kind of religion is Protestantism? 112
プロテスタントとはどのような宗教？

Q: What is the Mormon Church? 113
モルモン教とは？

Q: What kind of base does Catholicism have in the USA? 114
アメリカのカトリック人口は？

Q: Are there religious conflicts in the USA? 114
宗教による対立はあるの？

American Social Problems アメリカの社会問題 116

Q: How serious is the drug problem in the USA? 116
ドラッグの問題はどのくらい深刻か？

Q: What kinds of social problems does racial confrontation cause in the US? 117
人種の対立による社会問題はあるの？

Q: What is the status of gun control in the US? 118
銃の規制の現状は？

Q: What is the current state of crime in the US? 118
犯罪の現状は？

Q: How is the US unemployment rate changing? 119
失業率の推移は？

Family and Community 家庭とコミュニティ 120

Q: What kind of community activities are there in the US? 120
どんな地域コミュニティの活動があるの？

Q: What is the status of volunteer activity in the US? 121
ボランティア活動は行われているの？

Q: What are "family values"? 121
ファミリー・バリューとは？

Q: What is the real status of the breakdown of the family in the US? 123
家庭崩壊の現状は？

Q: Who is "Generation X"? 123
ジェネレーションXとは？

People and Nature 人と自然 125

Q: What does nature mean to Americans? 125
アメリカ人にとっての自然とは？

Q: What are the environmental pollution regulations in the US? 126
環境汚染の現状は？

Q: Why do Americans feel so much affection for dolphins and whales? 127
動物保護の実状は？

Chapter 6
Culture & Customs カルチャー＆カスタム 129

American Art アメリカのアート 130

Q: What was American art in the nineteenth century like? 130
19世紀のアメリカのアートとは？

Q: What were the main events in American art in the twentieth century? 131
20世紀のアメリカのアートとは？

Q: What is Pop art? 132
ポップアートとは？

American Entertainment and Show Business アメリカの映画産業とショービジネス 133

Q: How has Disney affected American culture? 133
ディズニーが与えた影響とは？

Q: How did the American movie industry develop? 134
映画産業の現状は？

Q: What is a Broadway musical? 135
ブロードウェイミュージカルとは？

American Music アメリカの音楽 136

Q: What is the history of American classical music? 136
クラシック音楽の歴史は？

Q: What is country music? 137
カントリー・ミュージックとは？

Q: How did Jazz and Blues develop? 138
ジャズやブルースはどのように発展したの？

Q: What is the generation of Rock 'n' Roll? 138
ロックンロール世代とは？

Q: How was "Rap" music created? 140
ラップミュージックとは？

National Culture and Regional Culture ナショナルカルチャーと地域文化 141

Q: Are there any cowboys left in America? 141
カウボーイは今もいる?

Q: What do Levi's jeans symbolize? 142
リーバイスが象徴するものとは?

Q: What kind of American culture does Las Vegas represent? 143
ラスベガスはどんな都市?

Food Culture 食文化 144

Q: Is Coca-Cola still representative of American food culture? 144
アメリカ人にとってのコカコーラとは?

Q: What is the national food of America? 145
アメリカ人の国民食とは?

Q: What is a "California Roll"? 146
カリフォルニア・ロールとは?

American Holidays アメリカの祝日 147

Q: What kind of events take place on Independence Day? 147
独立記念日とは?

Q: What is Martin Luther King, Jr. Day? 147
キング牧師の記念日とは?

Q: What kind of holidays are Memorial Day and Labor Day? 148
メモリアルデイとレーバーデイとは?

Q: What are the origins of Halloween? 148
ハロウィーンの起源は?

Q: What kind of holiday is Thanksgiving Day? 149
サンクス・ギビング・デイとは?

Q: What does Christmas mean to Americans? 150
クリスマス商戦はあるの?

Q: What are the Jewish holy days? 150
ユダヤ人の祝日とは?

American Sports アメリカのスポーツ 151

Q: What are the four major professional sports of America? 151
アメリカの4大プロスポーツとは？

Q: How popular is American football? 151
アメリカン・フットボールの人気は？

Q: Where does basketball get its mass of support? 152
バスケットボールが人気がある理由とは？

Q: Why hasn't soccer become more popular in the US? . 153
なぜサッカーは人気がないの？

Word List 156

【読み始める前に】

Chapter 1
まずはアメリカの基本的な情報についての知識をつけましょう。広大と言っても、具体的にアメリカはどのくらいの広さなのか、現在の50州はどのようにアメリカ合衆国に組み込まれて行ったのか。そしてアメリカといえば、移民の国。どんな国からやってきて、そして今、どういう力関係にあるのかなど、日本とは異なるお国事情を知りましょう。

- ☐ contiguous
- ☐ straddling
- ☐ impeded
- ☐ tributaries
- ☐ tectonic
- ☐ acclimatize
- ☐ inaugurated
- ☐ dispersed
- ☐ pejorative

Chapter 2
アメリカの歴史について英語で読み進めます。1775年から1783年までの8年間、アメリカ東部のイギリスの13植民地が、本国イギリスに対し、独立を勝ち取ろうと戦争を行います。さらに独立後のアメリカは、西部開拓、南北戦争、そして2つの世界大戦へと進んで行きます。

- ☐ undaunted
- ☐ confederation
- ☐ inception
- ☐ abhorred
- ☐ embarked
- ☐ secede
- ☐ deleterious
- ☐ revoke
- ☐ antagonistic

Chapter 3
民主党と共和党――この2大政党によるアメリカの政治システムとはどういうものか、また世界に大きな影響力を持つMr. President――アメリカ大統領の役割などのアメリカの政治にまつわる話のほかに、法体系、人権問題、内政・外交問題など、アメリカの今がわかります。

- ☐ emancipation
- ☐ promulgated
- ☐ quorum
- ☐ fluctuate
- ☐ interred
- ☐ staunchly
- ☐ endowed
- ☐ extenuating
- ☐ atrocious

Chapter 4
2008年9月に起きたリーマンショック。このアメリカのたった1社の投資銀行の破綻が、世界的な金融危機の引き金となったことは記憶に新しいところです。こうした多大な影響を与えうるアメリカの経済活動とはどういうものなのか。さらには世界をリードするアメリカ産業界の現状も興味のあるところです。

☐ devalued   ☐ exacerbated   ☐ apparatuses
☐ stagnation   ☐ proliferation   ☐ overapplication
☐ stipulates   ☐ disparity   ☐ discretion

Chapter 5
アメリカ社会や生活といった身近な質問に答えます。アメリカ人に人気のある町はどこか、どんなボランティア活動をしているのかといった質問から、タブー視、または話題としては敬遠されがちな宗教や同性愛者についても触れています。

☐ polarized   ☐ lobbied   ☐ precursors
☐ heresy   ☐ upheaval   ☐ adamant
☐ blatant   ☐ epitome   ☐ egregious

Chapter 6
多民族国家であるアメリカでは、クリスマスを祝う人、祝わない人それぞれで、自分の宗教に則った休日をとります。そんな祝日について解説をするほか、アメリカならではの音楽、アート、そしてスポーツについてよく聞かれる質問に答えています。ジーンズで有名なリーバイスはアメリカ人にとって何の象徴なのか？ そんなことが分かってくると、さらにアメリカを深く知ることができるかもしれません。

☐ imbued   ☐ reminiscent   ☐ debunked
☐ exuberantly   ☐ urbane   ☐ renditions
☐ epithet   ☐ permeated   ☐ disbanded

Chapter 1

The Land of the United States of America and Its People

USA Territory

Q: How large is the USA?

The total land area of the USA is 9,372,614 km^2, 25 times as much as Japan. The largest state is Alaska, which is 1,518,875 km^2, but the largest of the 48 contiguous states is Texas, which is 692,141 km^2 (1.83 times larger than Japan).

This vast land is inhabited by 307 million people, a number which is just over twice Japan's population.

Driving east to west on Interstate 80, which connects New York and San Francisco, the trip is 4,630 km. It takes a week to cross the continent by car. The same trip takes 6 hours by plane, and one hour less flying west to east with the prevailing westerly winds.

There is a 3-hour time difference between the East and West Coasts. This means that when commuters arrive at work in downtown San Francisco, New Yorkers are already having lunch.

Chapter 1 The Land of the United States of America and Its People

Q: When did USA territory gain its present form?

The United States of America is composed of fifty states. The most recent addition was Hawaii, which became a state in 1959.

The thirteen eastern states declared independence from Great Britain in 1776. In 1803, the vast prairie lands west of the Mississippi River were purchased from France.

The state of Texas, on the other hand, originally belonged to Mexico. The USA attained this state in a war with Mexico in 1845. California became a state in 1850.

The territory of mainland USA was fixed definitively when the region straddling present-day Arizona and New Mexico was purchased from Mexico in 1853 for $10 million, in order to construct the transcontinental railway. Alaska was purchased from Russia for only $7.2 million in 1867.

As these facts show, the USA is a country that consists of various states, each with its own origins and background. As a consequence, many states have developed their own unique governments and economic activities, which all contribute to the diversity from region to region.

Q: What are the areas, besides the 48 contiguous states, that compose the USA?

There are two other states besides the 48 contiguous states: Hawaii and Alaska. The USA also possesses many islands. The largest is Puerto Rico in the Caribbean Sea, which is treated similarly to a state, and whose residents have US citizenship. Some parts of the Virgin Islands to the west of Puerto Rico, and most of the Aleutian Islands to the east of Alaska, are American territories. The Mariana Islands, the largest of which are Guam and Saipan, and the Marshall Islands to the south of the Marianas, have been under the trust of the USA since WWII.

Geographical and Natural Features of the USA

Q: What are the USA's natural features?

Generally speaking, the East Coast is characterized by gently sloping hills and distinct changes of season.

The South has hot summers, and the farther south one goes, the more subtropical plants one will see. The central part of the USA (the Midwest) was originally a vast sweep of prairies, but it has now been made into farmland. To the north of the Midwest are many forests and lakes, and the climate is extremely cold in the winter and mild in the summer.

A vast desert area extends west of the Midwest across the Rocky Mountains. In the southern part of the desert, in Arizona, huge cacti grow, and the heat can be so extreme that fatalities occur. The northern part of the West, on the other hand, has extremely cold winters and steep mountains.

On the West Coast, the climate is generally mild. Mountains stretch down almost to the coastline in places. There are cedar forests in the north, and pines and cedars from the middle to the south of California, as well as prairies and steppes. In some areas, the desert almost reaches the coast.

Q: What kind of mountain ranges does the USA have?

The US has two "backbones," or mountain ridges, in the East and the West. In early times, when European settlers traveled inland from the East Coast, they found their passage impeded first by the Appalachian Mountains, which run north to south, then by deep forests and valleys.

Beyond Appalachia lies the plains of the Midwest. At the far end of the plains run the steep Rocky Mountains. Beyond the Rockies, going further west into the desert, one meets the Cascade Ranges in the north and the Sierra Nevada in the south, both as high as the Rockies. Beyond those ranges lies the Pacific Ocean.

The highest mountains in the US is in Alaska. Mt. McKinley, at 6,194 m above sea level, is the highest mountain in North America (ranked 35th in the world). The highest mountain in the 48 contiguous states is Mt. Whitney in California, at 4,418 m.

Q: What kind of lakes are the Great Lakes?

These five huge lakes gathered in a cluster at the US-Canada border were formed when the ice of the Ice Age melted. They are the largest group of fresh-water lakes in the world, extending from the state of Minnesota in the West to the state of New York in the East.

Their names are, from west to east, Lake Superior, Michigan, Huron, Erie and Ontario. Lake Superior is the second largest lake in the world next to the Caspian Sea. At 82,414 km² it is one-third

The five Great Lakes make up the biggest group of fresh-water lakes in the world.

CHAPTER 1 THE LAND OF THE UNITED STATES OF AMERICA AND ITS PEOPLE

the size of Japan's Honshu Island. Lake Huron is the fifth largest in the world, Lake Michigan the sixth, and Lake Erie and Ontario the eleventh and fifteenth.

All the Great Lakes are connected with each other, either directly or indirectly via rivers. From Lake Ontario, which is the easternmost body of water, the St. Lawrence River extends into the Atlantic Ocean. From Lake Erie it is possible to transport goods to New York via rivers and canals. It is possible to go all the way down to the Gulf of Mexico via the Mississippi River.

The regions around the Great Lakes were thus an important hub of transportation from early times. Big cities like Buffalo, Detroit, and Chicago from the end of the 19th century onwards functioned as distribution and manufacturing centers for the USA.

Q: What kind of river is the Mississippi?

It is said that when the Mississippi River rages, the cost of meat in Japanese supermarkets goes up. Why? Because the corn fields stretching along the river produce cornfeed for Japanese livestock.

The Mississippi flows down from the lake areas in

The Mississippi River is an important waterway for the transportation of goods.

Minnesota into the Gulf of Mexico. The word Mississippi means "Father of the Waters" in the Native American Chippewa language, and the USA is divided into east and west by this river. In the frontier period, it was relatively easy to travel from the East Coast as far as the river. To "go west" actually meant to travel beyond it.

In the nineteenth century, steamboats plied the river, carrying goods and people. On either side lie stretches of fertile plains—corn fields in the north, cotton fields in the south. To the west there are long stretches of pastures and granaries. The freight volume transported along the Mississippi and its tributaries amounts to almost 60% of total water transport in the USA. The Mississippi River actually functions as a main artery supplying the American Continent.

The total length of the Mississippi, including its longest tributary, the Missouri, is 6,210 km. This makes it the fourth longest river in the world, after the Nile, the Amazon, and the Chang Jiang.

Q: What kind of national parks does the USA have?

The USA has 58 national parks. Areas with remarkable natural scenery and views or resources that are scientifically, geologically, or biologically invaluable are designated as national parks, and are protected under the management of the federal government. These parks are open to the public. The first national park was designated in 1872. It was Yellowstone National Park, which extends over the states of Wyoming, Montana, and Idaho.

Yellowstone National Park is America's first national park.

The most notable characteristic of American national parks is their huge scale. The Grand Canyon has a total length of 450 km; Yellowstone is as large as two Yamanashi prefectures. People often spend several days at a time at these parks, enjoying the vastness of nature during their vacations.

The Climate of the USA

Q: What are the characteristics of the American climate?

The USA comprises a vast area of land, so almost every kind of climate can be observed. Among the 48 contiguous states, the hottest zone is the desert area that stretches across Arizona, southern Nevada, and inland California, where the temperature sometimes rises to over 50°C. In 1913, a temperature of 57°C was recorded in California's Death Valley.

The coldest zone is the USA-Canada border from Montana to Minnesota. Montana holds the record −56.5°C in 1954.

Q: Do tornadoes really occur in various places?

Tornadoes have been known to occur almost everywhere in the USA. They are most likely to occur during the strong thunderstorms from spring to summer. Since tornadoes can cause serious damage and hundreds of fatalities, meteorologists continue to research how to accurately predict their occurrence.

Tornadoes occur particularly in inland areas like Kansas, Nebraska, Oklahoma, or Texas. These states are known collectively as "Tornado Alley." An average of 153 tornadoes touch down in Texas each year, making it the state with the most tornadoes in the US. These regions have instruction billboards showing people specific buildings to escape to in the case of a tornado. Buildings with sturdy central structures make safe evacuation sites.

CHAPTER 1 THE LAND OF THE UNITED STATES OF AMERICA AND ITS PEOPLE

Q: Does the USA have earthquakes like Japan?

Earthquakes take place mostly on the West Coast, around the San Andreas fault, which extends for 950 km where the Pacific and the American Continental tectonic plates meet.

The San Francisco earthquake of 1906 is particularly well known. It measured 8.3 on the Richter scale, caused 478 deaths, and engulfed most of the city in fire. Another earthquake hit San Francisco in 1989, just when the city was caught up in the excitement of the Superbowl, the final game in the season for American football. That quake, the Loma Prieta, was so violent it caused freeways to snap into two.

But other areas are not necessarily any safer. Charleston, the old capital of South Carolina, was hit by an earthquake of 7.7 magnitude in 1886. In 1811, a large earthquake was recorded in Missouri, the central part of the USA.

Q: How is a hurricane different from a typhoon?

Hurricanes are generated over the Atlantic Ocean. They are intense tropical depressions that attack the East Coast from summer into autumn. The hurricane is, so to speak, an American typhoon. The areas that are most frequently hit are known as Hurricane

Alleys. They consist of the coastal regions from Florida to North Carolina on the Atlantic, and from Texas to Florida on the Gulf of Mexico.

The most violent hurricane ever recorded was the one that attacked Galveston, Texas, at the end of August and into September in 1900: more than 6,000 people were killed. More recently, in 2005, Louisiana, Mississippi, Alabama, and Florida was hit by Hurricane Katrina.

Incidentally, in the past hurricanes were given women's names, a practice that derived from the stereotyped idea that women easily become emotional and hysterical. These days, men's names are also used to avoid gender discrimination. Thus, even the naming of hurricanes has been influenced by social change.

The People of America

Q: How has the American population changed?

The American population topped the 300 million

mark in 2006. Currently the figure is 307 million.

When people started settling in America on a large scale in the early seventeenth century (from 1620 onwards), it is said that approximately 2,300 people inhabited America. By the Civil War (1770) the population had grown to 2.14 million, and by the beginning of the nineteenth century, 5.3 million. By the beginning of the twentieth century, it had reached 76 million—and the 1920 census exceeded 100 million. In just three hundred years, the number of people who had immigrated to the USA and multiplied there had reached huge proportions. The population is expected to exceed 400 million in 2050.

Q: What kinds of people emigrated to the USA from Europe?

From the start, the USA has accepted immigrants from all over the world and has expanded accordingly. That principle will never change.

The first to come were the British, Dutch, and Spanish, who also brought their black slaves. Next came the Irish, Germans, and Italians, followed by Jews from Russia and Eastern Europe.

The early settlers were people who had come over for religious regions, in order to make a living. Many of them thought of America as a new world, a land God had given them to develop. There were also many fur merchants who came to America to export fur to Europe.

After the mid-nineteenth century, the number of immigrants seeking refuge for economical or political reasons such as poverty or persecution increased. For example, the great potato famine in Ireland in 1846 brought many hungry and poor Irish over to the East Coast.

The next wave of immigrants consisted of people from Germany, driven by fear of the political situation. From the end of the nineteenth century many Jews fled from Russia and Eastern Europe to avoid persecution. Italians also came as seasonal workers. The city populations quickly swelled with their numbers. Immigrants who had savings moved inland to develop the countryside.

Even now, there are many Europeans immigrating to the USA. Immigrants from Eastern Europe and Russia in particular are increasing.

Q: What phenomenon does the term "Asian Power" refer to?

The first Asian immigrants to the USA were Chinese. They came to the West Coast in the mid-nineteenth century during the time of the Gold Rush. They worked as servants, miners, and tracklayers in railway construction. Later, the Japanese immigrated into

Hawaii and the West Coast as farmers.

As Asian immigrants increased, threatening the occupations of the whites who had long resided in those areas, anti-Japanese and anti-Chinese movements formed, leading to the establishment of a law to limit immigration from Japan and China. Immigration from Asia remained at the same low level until the law was abolished.

New York's Chinatown is a vibrant Asian immigrant community.

Recent years have seen a new influx of Asian immigrants. It includes Chinese from Hong Kong, Taiwan and mainland China, Koreans, Southeast Asians such as Vietnamese, and immigrants from India and Bangladesh. They pour into East and West Coast cities. There are, for example, as many as 400,000 Chinese and Southeast Asians living in New York's Chinatown.

They are losing no time in making inroads into American society and attracting attention as a new, strong power in the USA.

Q: What is the current ethnic make-up of the USA population?

It is fair to say that the USA is inhabited by people from all over the world.

Interestingly, many of the cab drivers in Midwestern cities are Ethiopian. On the coast of the Gulf of Mexico in Texas, on the other hand, one can see many Vietnamese fishermen. San Francisco and New York both have extensive Chinatowns.

Mexicans and Central Americans are also pouring into Southern California. Many of them are "illegal aliens," and the source of headaches for immigration officials. However, many of the officers themselves are also immigrants from Mexico or Asia.

America is becoming increasingly diversified and colorful. In some companies in Silicon Valley, engineers from countries such as Russia and India exceed the number of US engineers. At present, the number of first-generation Americans born out of the USA is 12.1% of the total population. According to the 2010 US Census, the non-white population will exceed the white by the year 2050.

With all these changes, many people worry that the USA will lose its traditional identity. These people demand stricter laws to curb the influx of immigrants. However, as long as conflict, poverty, and political oppression exist in the world, and as long as America offers the dream of affluence and freedom, people will continue to set out for the New World.

CHAPTER 1 THE LAND OF THE UNITED STATES OF AMERICA AND ITS PEOPLE

Q: What kind of people make up the white population in America?

The white population in the USA originates from various places in Europe. According to a 2010 census, the largest segment is from Germany, at 42.8 million. These are followed by the Irish, at 30.5 million. Those from England number 24.5 million, and those from Italy, 15.6 million.

The religious background of the white population varies as well: German and British descendants are typically Protestant, while Irish and Italian are typically Catholic. But there are many other religions besides Christianity. For example, there are also Jews, with different cultural traditions.

Much of the Polish population (8.9 million in total) is concentrated in Chicago. In no other city in the world except Warsaw can one see so many Polish residents living together.

Descendants of Irish immigrants are now widely integrated into American society. Once, however, they were so poor that they suffered discrimination from other white groups. At one time it was common to see "No Irish" printed in many classified advertisements in newspapers. Many Irish immigrants originally fled poverty and the oppressive political situation in Ireland when it was a British colony. Like the Italians, who are also Catholic, they entered American society at the lowest level and endured hardships to gain success.

Q: Who does the word "WASP" refer to?

WASP is a slang abbreviation for White Anglo-Saxon Protestant, a phrase that refers to the descendants of the British who came to America, lived in New England, and played a leading role in the history of American independence. After the War of Independence, WASPs exerted a strong influence in the formation of culture and values as the American majority. They eventually became the mainstream in the political and economic arenas.

As a consequence, the first step for later immigrants was to acclimatize themselves to the WASP lifestyle and values. This tendency is still obvious. All the American presidents before John F. Kennedy (inaugurated in 1960) had WASP backgrounds.

At present, immigrants come not only from Europe, but from all over the world. And Catholics form a good proportion of those immigrants who are Christian.

Q: What kind of influence have people from Latin countries had in the USA?

Latinos, that is to say people from Central and South

America, have been immigrating to America since early times. The number of people in the states who speak Spanish is as high as 45 million. If we count the number of people who are already naturalized, some 35.62 million Latinos live in the USA.

In New York, a city inhabited by many Caribbean and South American people, subway announcements and advertisements are often made in Spanish. Latino culture and lifestyle have penetrated deeply into America, with Latino food and art. Spanish is second only to English as the most widely spoken language in the States. The number of Spanish-speaking immigrants is only expected to keep growing.

Q: Which people does the word "blacks" refer to?

Currently, there are approximately 40.45 million black people in the USA. They have various roots. Many of their ancestors were originally brought from Africa or the Caribbean, but recently there has been a fresh wave of immigrants from Africa. Over the course of American history, the word "black" also included mulattos or their children.

There are black populations dispersed all over the States, but particularly in the South. The majority are the descendants of Africans forced to come to the United States as slaves. It was not only in the South that the system of slavery existed: until the beginning of the nineteenth century, buying and selling slaves was also permitted in the North. The total number of slaves brought to America is thought to have totaled 10 to 12 million—a startling figure. Due to poor traveling conditions at sea and to mutinies, at least 2 million people are estimated to have died, either on the way or upon arrival.

The South maintained the system of slavery until the end of the Civil War, which is why a large population of blacks is still concentrated there. This is particularly true in the states of Mississippi, where 37% of the total population is black, and Louisiana, where the number is 32%. It was only in 1964 that the rights of black people came under equal protection by law. It was at this time that civil rights laws that prohibited discrimination by race or gender were passed.

At present, blacks comprise the third largest ethnic group in America. Their political power cannot be ignored, and they are a core group in human rights and discrimination issues.

Q: What is the social status of blacks in the USA?

Since the period of slavery, large numbers of black people have been forced to live at the lowest

CHAPTER 1 THE LAND OF THE UNITED STATES OF AMERICA AND ITS PEOPLE

levels of society. Even after their equality had been guaranteed under law, they are still beset by serious economic disadvantages. A vicious cycle is created, as poor blacks live in inner-city slums and conditions deteriorate, giving rise to more prejudice and worse ethnic conflict.

Black culture can be credited with producing Jazz and Blues music, recognized worldwide and often taken as representing the culture of America. Numerous black people have taken active roles in the center of American life—in 2008, Barack Obama became the first African American president of the United States. The percentage of black people with high educational backgrounds is increasing.

These days, many people use the term "African American" instead of "black." The word "Negro" is also considered pejorative since it was originally used when discrimination was the norm.

Q: What is the real meaning of "Jewish Power"?

The term "Jewish" does not refer to any one specific ethnic group, but rather to all the peoples gathered under the religion of Judaism. In the USA, the term includes the descendants of these early immigrants.

Jews came to the East Coast very early on and engaged in commerce and trade. Countries like

England and Holland, which had power and influence over America in the seventeenth and eighteenth centuries, had adopted open policies toward Jews in order to promote business. A considerable amount of Jewish financial capital thus flowed into America from the early years.

Immigration of Jews into America on a large scale, however, only began about 120 years ago. This was a time when many Jews were fleeing persecution in Russia and Eastern Europe, and they arrived in America with only the clothes on their backs. They took up work in tailoring and other trades, enduring great poverty.

But discrimination against Jews, which had persisted for centuries in Europe, also found its way into America. Even in the New World, Jews became subject to discrimination and persecution.

Many Jewish people have therefore chosen to live all together in urban areas with less fear of persecution. In a 1930 census, 25% of the New York population, and 65% of those engaged in the legal profession, were said to be Jewish.

Jews also played a prominent part in the big movie industries in Hollywood. The Jews are one of the most successful groups of immigrants in the USA.

A large population of Jewish immigrants have become successful in America.

CHAPTER 1 THE LAND OF THE UNITED STATES OF AMERICA AND ITS PEOPLE

Q: Why are Indians called Native Americans?

The indigenous people of America were once called Indians, but now it is customary to refer to term as "Native Americans." The name "Indian" derives from Christopher Columbus's mistaken belief that he had discovered India when he came to America. To some, the name is an embodiment of white immigrant oppression of the indigenous people.

The term Native American is therefore symbolic of the awareness that these are the native peoples of America.

After the 1960s, a movement to assert the rights of Native Americans grew up, and it led to the abolishment of much long-standing discrimination and oppression. The word "Native American" is an expression of the success of this campaign. Native American culture was widely publicized as a result, and their ways of thinking and practical wisdom exerted considerable influence over the New Age movement. Nevertheless, having existed on the edge of society for so many years, Native Americans are still beset by a serious problem of

Native Americans were the original inhabitants of North America.

poverty. The Native American population is expected to reach 5.4 million by the mid twenty-first century. Improving their standard of living while maintaining their traditions remains their primary challenge.

Q: How have relations between Native Americans and other Americans changed?

It is said that Native Americans immigrated to America more than 15,000 years ago, across the Bering Sea. It is estimated that about 2 million Native Americans inhabited the USA in the sixteenth century, when the first European settlers arrived on a large scale. There were Native Americans all over the USA in various tribes speaking more than 1,000 languages.

Native Americans were generally quite welcoming when the first Europeans arrived. However, many native tribes died from epidemics brought by the settlers. Confrontation increased as the number of whites increased. Native Americans found themselves embroiled in the eighteenth-century struggle between French and English sovereignty in the New World. The British Army even distributed blankets infected with smallpox germs to Native Americans.

As is well known, Native Americans were pushed into desperate circumstances as the Western Frontier moved ever westward in the course of the nineteenth century. By the end of the century the Native American population had declined sharply, to around 240,000.

Q: What influences did Americans receive from Native Americans?

European immigrants adopted some of the customs and communication methods of Native Americans from early times.

One such custom was the tribal meeting, originally conducted by the Iroquois tribe, who lived all over the Northeast. It is said that at the time of the Civil War American leaders used ideas from the Iroquois system in drawing up the kind of democratic government they themselves wanted. The American way of looking one's speaking partner straight in the eye and asserting oneself in a loud voice is also said to have been fostered during exchanges with Native Americans.

It is also a fact that in the twentieth century, as the simple lifestyle of Native Americans became more widely known, their arts, crafts, rituals, and traditions exerted a tremendous influence on American art.

Q: What does the word "diversity" mean?

Diversity is an English word meaning "variety," and it has very positive nuances.

America is a country composed of various groups of immigrants. It is, literally, a country of diversity. Its people present a variety of competing ideas, which provide the country's source of energy.

Nowadays, there is an extraordinary number of different ethnic groups in the USA, and they must all co-exist. "Diversity" has become one of the most important values in America.

"Diversity" is an extension of the phrase "melting pot," with the positive nuances stressed. It refers to the fact that people can make the USA their own country, even while they maintain their ethnic identities.

The former mayor of New York, David Dinkins, once made a famous comment; he described diversity as a "beautiful mosaic." As the phrase indicates, diversity is a word that has strong appeal for American society, a nation composed of many different people, with various racial and cultural backgrounds.

Q: Is English the national language in the USA?

There is in fact no law stipulating that English is the national language of the USA. There are as many as 55 million Americans whose mother tongue is another language altogether, and who speak English as a second language. They amount to 20% of the total population, and are concentrated in urban areas.

In some Californian elementary schools, the number of Central American children has increased so much that classes are offered in Spanish rather than English. English-speaking children learn Spanish to have more chance of making friends with Spanish-speaking children.

But apart from urban areas on the East and West Coasts, and if one excepts the Southwest with its large population of Mexican-Americans, most of the country is English-speaking. This is a large factor in the difference between urban provincial areas as living environments.

The Differences in Regions in the USA

Q: What kind of region is New England?

New England is a region in the northeast of the USA consisting of six states: Massachusetts, Maine, Vermont, New Hampshire, Rhode Island, and Connecticut. The largest city is Boston, with a population of 570,000 (21st in the USA). The total population of New England is 13,206,000.

New England was so named by John Smith, the famous explorer who founded the Virginia colony. He explored the area in 1614. Later, when the Pilgrims came across the Atlantic in the Mayflower, they moved into Plymouth, Massachusetts. It was then that New England began to develop. It is one of the oldest colonies in North America.

The Pilgrims tried to create colonies in a very harsh environment, and half of the first settlers did not survive the first winter.

The spirit of New England consists of diligence, enthusiasm for education, respect for public welfare, and active volunteering, all of which derive from the old Protestant tradition of the Pilgrims. In its promotional material the state of Massachusetts states that "the heart of Massachusetts is the heart of America," emphasizing the traditionalism of the region.

Q: Do New York and Los Angeles represent East and West Coast cultures?

New York, the largest industrial city in the East, and Los Angeles, the largest urban area in California, each represent East Coast and West Coast characteristics, and they are rather like rivals.

CHAPTER 1 THE LAND OF THE UNITED STATES OF AMERICA AND ITS PEOPLE

New York is a city that has an old history and tradition, while Los Angeles is a huge urban area that developed rapidly during the twentieth century.

For example, whereas show business in New York consists of Broadway musicals, Los Angeles has Hollywood movies made with gigantic sets and studio locations.

New Yorkers travel by subway and on foot, while Los Angeleans drive the freeways, park their cars in lots under palm trees, and go to their offices in colorful Mexican-style buildings.

The climates differ greatly as well. One needs a coat and muffler when boarding a plane in the New York winter, but arriving at LAX airport during the same season, all one needs is a shirt.

In New York, one can see many immigrants from Europe, the Caribbean, and Asia in the working population in the city. In LA one sees various Asians, a lot of Mexicans, and European immigrants.

Los Angeles and New York are the largest cities on the West and East Coasts, respectively.

Thus, not only are the East and West Coasts geographically separate, they also have very different regional characteristics.

Q: What is the Midwest, or the "Heartland," like as a region?

The region right at the center of the USA is called the Heartland. It is a vast plain beyond the Appalachian Mountains that extends all the way to the Rockies. People call this vast region the Midwest (though this does not cover the South), but its nickname is the Heartland. The Mississippi and its numerous tributaries spread out over the Heartland like a fan.

This region is predominantly farmland: there is a lot of corn, wheat, and dairy farming. Roads go straight on, seemingly without end, without a mountain or hill in sight. The area is noted for its rich greenery, harsh winters, and hot summers, as well as torrential thunderstorms. Tornadoes also hit the region from time to time.

The inhabitants of the Heartland are descendants of the people who cultivated this vast land and developed its agriculture—mostly European Protestant immigrants. Many of them have simple and conservative lifestyles.

CHAPTER 1　THE LAND OF THE UNITED STATES OF AMERICA AND ITS PEOPLE

Q: What kind of region is the South?

Crossing the Potomac river after Washington, D.C., one arrives in the state of Virginia. Virginia is a part of the South, a region that, no doubt, many people associate with the movie "Gone with the Wind."

The South was one of the first regions to be colonized. Soon after Independence, however, the Southern economy was greatly affected by industry and financial developments in the North. Opposition against the economic control of the North led to the Civil War.

A strong Southern pride is still evident in the South. This pride is related to the struggle against the North. In Atlanta, Georgia, one can see the imposing bronze statue of General Lee, the Commander-in-Chief of the Confederate Army.

After the Civil War, a dark image haunted the South. It was seen as lagging behind the North economically, and as a place where racial discrimination still existed long after slaves were liberated.

Southerners speak English with striking accents, and the Southern weather and climate is mild. These elements, coupled with a kind temperament, referred to as "Southern Hospitality," as well as delicious regional dishes such as Cajun cooking, all contribute to its appeal for tourists.

The South's total population is 109 million. The largest population is in Florida (18.5 million). The South is one of the most promising regions in the USA and is expected to continue to grow as a base of American industry.

Chapter 2

History and Background of the USA

National Anthem and Flag

Q: What is the national anthem of the USA?

"The Star-Spangled Banner" was officially adopted as the national anthem in March 1931, but the song actually dates from the early nineteenth century. The Napoleonic Wars in Europe provided the spark that caused America to open hostilities against England in 1812. The war continued until 1814, and it was a tough battle for America. British troops even got as far as invading Washington, D.C. at one time during the conflict.

The words to "The Star-Spangled Banner" come from a patriotic poem composed by the American lawyer Francis Scott Key. Confined in a British warship, he was moved to write the poem when he caught sight of a Star-Spangled banner still fluttering beyond the smoke, undaunted by the British gunfire.

The poem soon became very popular in the USA, but the tune actually came from a British song, "To Anacreon in Heaven," popularly sung in English taverns.

The composer was John Stafford Smith. It is amusing to think that what became the American national anthem borrowed its original tune from a country against whom it had fought a war.

Q: What is the history of the design of American flag?

As everybody knows, the American flag is composed of stars, which indicate the number of states. The red and blue stripes represent the thirteen states at the time of Independence.

One of the first designs of the national flag did not feature any stars.

During colonial times, no specific format for a flag existed other than that the stars were usually arranged in a circle. Since there was no set standard, freely designed flags were used for public events.

At first this was quite satisfactory. Then, Vermont and Kentucky joined the Confederation in 1791 and 1792 respectively, and the number of stars and stripes increased to fifteen. As still more states joined, Congress decided in 1818 that only the first thirteen states would be shown as stripes, and the total number of states would be shown as stars.

The American flag is a symbol of the process the USA underwent in the course of its construction as a nation; state after state was added once Independence had been gained. The current flag with fifty stars was designed in 1959 when Hawaii became the fiftieth state in the USA.

The History of the USA

Q: How old is America?

America declared independence from England in 1776, so it has been only about 235 years since America was founded as a nation. Official acknowledgment as an independent country by other countries, however, was not made until 1783. If one counts that date as its inception, the USA is even younger as a country.

This relative youth is one reason why the USA developed quickly to become a world power in a short period of time. It was unrestricted by old customs or traditions.

However, one should not forget a nation consisting

Chapter 2 History and Background of the USA

of numerous tribes of Native Americans existed in North America from well before Independence. It was approximately 20,000 years ago that Native Americans first settled in the States. If one takes this fact into consideration, a much older culture existed in America that provided the starting point for the nation.

Q: What was America like before Independence?

It was at the end of the fifteenth century that Europeans first gained access to America, the land of the Native Americans. Columbus made his famous voyage to the West Indies in 1492. Later, in the sixteenth century, numerous explorers landed in North America and introduced the New Continent to Spain, England, and Holland.

Full-scale settlement started in the early seventeenth century. British and Dutch settled mostly in the East Coast; Spanish settled in the South and also in present-day Texas; French settled in an area stretching from the Gulf of Mexico further inland.

Many of the settlers were fleeing religious persecution in Europe, or had been officially sent by the major European powers. For example, New York originated when the Dutch opened a colony called New Amsterdam in lower Manhattan in the early sixteenth century. In 1650, 1,500 people lived in New Amsterdam, speaking fifteen different languages.

Various groups of Europeans with diverse backgrounds had thus come to the East and the South to settle before the War of Independence. They developed the land, creating villages and running colonies in their own styles.

The settlers lived in clusters all over the vast continent. Though they pledged loyalty to their mother country or their sovereign state of England, they did not hope to be a unified colony, nor were they even aware of themselves as such.

This early tradition of independence became the origin of the common American view, which holds true even today, that regional governments should establish their own laws and institutions, and central government should be limited.

Q: How did America decide to become independent?

The War of Independence had its origins in the French and Indian Wars fought between England and France over control of North American territories—wars in which Native Americans too were involved. England won, but the British government then tried to recoup war expenses by raising settlers' taxes. In an effort to assert its authority, Britain also prohibited settlers from moving beyond the Appalachian Mountains. The settlers rebelled, and this led to the War of Independence.

The settlers were particularly upset by England's unilateral tax imposition, which they viewed as an abuse of the rights of a colony since it had no representation in the British Parliament. Demonstrations grew particularly intense in Boston, and tension rose. England counteracted by force, depriving the settlers of weapons. This was the direct cause of the war.

Q: What were the various stages in the War of Independence (The American Revolution)?

At the start of the war, the colonial troops, which had been hastily prepared, suffered one defeat after another at the hands of British troops. Not all of the settlers desired independence, and many of them found it difficult to discard their loyalty to England.

England, however, found it difficult to make the best use of pro-British settlers in the colonies. It also failed on a diplomatic level—its rival France ended up supporting the colonies and participating in the war. England began suffering defeats and the tables turned. The Revolutionary Army, led by George Washington, gained its full power, and the thirteen states of America were finally acknowledged as an independent nation at the Peace Conference in Paris.

Q: What situation did America find itself in after independence?

America finally obtained its independence at the 1783 Treaty of Paris, obtaining all the territory east of the Mississippi. But much discussion still remained on how the country, previously just a loose conglomeration of people, was to build itself into a nation.

The problem was persuading the colonists, who had fought hard for their freedom and abhorred strong government, of the need to establish a new central government. Many people wanted to manage their own towns or villages, and held suspicions about a strong central government.

Confrontation continued for a while between those who held regional autonomy in high regard, and those who supported the Confederation. In 1801 the confrontation intensified when the third President, Thomas Jefferson, a Republican, supported regional autonomy, while the Federalists, led by Alexander Hamilton, supported the Confederation.

Support for strong government is still reflected in the views of contemporary Democrats. The assertion of the rights of the individual and the autonomy of local governments is reflected in the modern Republican Party. American public opinion is divided in this way all the time. The small government advocated by former president Ronald Reagan and

Chapter 2 History and Background of the USA

the strengthening of the role of central government as represented by former president Clinton's Health and Social Welfare Plan can both be traced back to arguments originating at the time of Independence.

Q: When did westward development start in America?

During the period from the War of Independence to the beginning of the nineteenth century, the word "West" meant west of the Appalachian Mountains, which run south to north in the East.

It was the Spanish who first explored the vast lands to the west of these Appalachian Mountains. Later, in the seventeenth century, the French colonized and cultivated the area. They opened a colony called Louisiana, or "the land of the Louis Dynasty." This vast land extended south to New Orleans and north to the Canadian border along the Mississippi River, and west to the Rockies. America purchased it at an extremely good price in 1803 from Napoleon, who badly needed to raise money for his war in Europe. With the Louisiana purchase, westward development could begin at last.

An 1849 ad promotes California as a land of opportunity.

Around 1830, a huge number of pioneers moved westward looking for fertile land, and the frontier moved westward accordingly.

The boundary between the West Coast, which had started being developed from 1849 with the Gold Rush, and the frontier, which the settlers from the East had been gradually pushing westward, finally disappeared around 1890.

Q: When was Texas incorporated into the USA?

Texas gained independence from Mexico in 1836. American settlers from the southeast had already moved into Texas and established cotton plantations from around 1820. Their number had increased to 22,000 (2,000 of which were slaves) by 1830. These people were Protestants and unwelcome to the Mexicans who were Catholic and had Spanish traditions. There were only about 1,000 Mexicans in the area, and they felt severely outnumbered.

Mexico soon took measures to prohibit American settlement, so American settlers rose up against Mexico to fight for independence in 1835. The most famous event during the ensuing war was the fight to the death by men who had been holed up in a mission called the Alamo in San Antonio. The story of this incident has been handed down from generation to generation, along with the slogan "Remember the Alamo." A famous movie starring John Wayne was made about this incident.

In 1845, Texas defeated Mexico, won its independence, and was incorporated into the USA. Houston was named after Sam Houston, one of the heroes who led the war.

Q: What was the Oregon Trail?

From 1830 to 1860, one out of fifty Americans embarked on a journey along an unmarked trail toward Portland, Oregon. In those days, Oregon had fertile farmlands, which were offered free to cultivators. Countless people trying to put lives of poverty in the East behind them and looking for a chance to attain wealth gathered at a town called Independence, east of Kansas City. They were brought there from the East via boats and other means.

West of Independence lay a wild, uncultivated region. The total distance from Independence to Oregon was 3,500 km. It was a journey that could be advanced at only 15 km a day, since the

A typical "covered wagon" used on the Oregon Trail.

travelers dragged oxcarts full of food and household belongings. They used oxcarts because oxen subsist on grass and were therefore good for the harsh journey, and they could become food in an emergency. The journey took six months: the travelers endured the hardships of nature and defended themselves against attacks from Native Americans. They left in spring because they had to cross the mountains in the West before the snow season.

In those days, countless people challenged the frontier, traveling to the West to take part in the California Gold Rush. So many people left Independence in the early spring that the area was said to be covered in a thick cloud of dust. Their covered wagons going west over the plains were called "prairie schooners."

Q: What was the Civil War about?

The Civil War started when eleven Southern states, all of whom had been left behind economically by the Northeast, tried to secede from the USA in an attempt to keep hold of the system of slavery.

By this time, the industrial revolution had already progressed considerably. Consequently, weapon precision had increased and machine guns had been introduced. But there was a large gap between weaponry and strategy, which led to many fatalities

Chapter 2 History and Background of the USA

A depiction of the Battle of Gettysburg, a famous battle during the Civil War.

in battle. In the four years from 1861 to 1865, 623,000 were killed—the greatest war casualties America had ever experienced. Both South and North openly recruited soldiers from Europe with the promise of granting them citizenship.

The South eventually surrendered, and the damage it sustained from the war had a deleterious effect on its economy well into the twentieth century. The war proved that it was impossible to secede from the confederation by force. Thereafter, the nation turned its full attention to development of the West.

The Civil War was one of the most important events in American history in that it was the starting point for all the states to come together to begin development as a nation.

Q: When did development start in California?

The West Coast in and around California had been discovered and gradually settled by Spanish explorers in the seventeenth century. California has many Spanish place names, reminders of these Spanish settlements and of later Mexican occupation.

However, it was only after 1848, when gold was discovered and the Gold Rush took place, that large populations began to settle in California. In ten years, hundreds of thousand of people came by land and sea to settle, overwhelming the Native Americans and Mexicans who had already made it their home.

This is only one example in American history where settlers moved into the wilderness and took it over, overwhelming the natives already living there through sheer numbers.

California became an American territory in 1848, as a consequence of the Mexican War. After that, it rapidly became Americanized as settler activity proceeded.

Incidentally, people who took part in the California Gold Rush are referred to as "Forty-Niners," after the year (1849) in which the Gold Rush reached its peak. Nowadays, the term is also the name of the San Francisco pro-football team.

The opening of the Transcontinental Railway

Chapter 2 History and Background of the USA

accelerated West Coast development.

Q: Why has America shown so much growth in the twentieth century?

The tremendous growth America has shown in the twentieth century is undoubtedly due to the spirit and energy of its huge number of immigrants and their offspring. In the nineteenth century alone, the North American population grew fourteen times to total 76 million at the start of the twentieth century. All those people were engaged in the development of the country, so their power was absolutely enormous.

They all made every effort to grasp success and pull themselves out of poverty with their own hands, engaging in new enterprises and inventions. It was at the beginning of the twentieth century that their efforts began to bear fruit. The invention of the telephone by Alexander Graham Bell, who had immigrated to the USA via Canada from England, led to the development of an enterprise. America gained leadership thereafter in the telecommunications industry. Macy's department store developed in New York at the same time. Macy's was originally a successful general store run in the nineteenth century by an ex-whaler—he used the design of the tattoo on his arm as the store's logo. During this same period, Thomas Edison, the son of a poor lumber dealer with a brilliant talent for invention, developed a succession of electrical products that made the American electronics industry a leader in the twentieth century.

This kind of "American dream" continued to rapidly bear fruit. Successful people invested further money in new ideas, which pushed the American economy to expand even more. People sought frantically to create opportunities by doing something that no one else was doing. This helped develop a particularly American attitude that one reaches success by promoting unique and totally original ideas.

During this period from the end of the nineteenth century to the early twentieth century while America was growing steadily, the various countries of Europe were either coming into conflict with one another or undergoing civil war as their old orders fell. Thus America's position rose as the situation in Europe became less stable.

By the time WWI broke out, America had become a world economic power.

Q: What did WWI mean for the USA?

WWI brought devastation to Europe. But it also led the USA, now a mighty nation, to obtain a decisive influence over world events. The sinking of an American vessel by an all-out attack by a German submarine

Chapter 2 History and Background of the USA

led the USA to revoke its stance of neutrality and participate in the war in Europe. Thus, the USA attained influential power in the international arena.

After the war, the USA remained outside the League of Nations and kept its distance from European politics. However, the USA was the world's largest creditor nation, and its economy comprised 25% of the world's GDP. The USA maintains the same figure in the world economy now.

Q: What led the USA to join WWII?

The Great Depression, triggered by the stock-market crash on Wall Street in 1929, dealt a hard blow to the USA. The streets teemed with unemployed workers.

The New York Stock Exchange after the crash of 1929.

What was more surprising was the blow the Depression dealt to the world at large. It proved that the American economy was so powerful it could send reverberations to other countries. Notwithstanding the Depression, however, in 1931 the Empire State Building was completed and construction began on the Rockefeller Center. In 1933, construction of the Golden Gate Bridge started in San Francisco. The American economy began to recover around this time under the leadership of President Theodore Roosevelt.

It is well known that the Depression brought

instability to Europe and the Far East. When the USA took a firm stance against the Japanese invasion of China, US-Japan relations worsened day by day. The USA also opposed the war started by Germany and built an alliance with England. At the beginning of World War II, Americans held fast to their belief that their country should keep out of other nations' conflicts and look to her own security and prosperity. At this point, therefore, the USA was not directly involved. What brought the USA into the war was Japan's opening of hostilities—the sudden Japanese attack on the US military base in Pearl Harbor.

Q: What impact did the Vietnam War have on the USA?

The Vietnam War was a war in which the USA, still reveling in its post-world-war glory, took its first bad stumble. Having intervened in the dispute of another country in an attempt to defend "Pax Americana," it became hopelessly mired, and a lot of young Americans lost their lives. The surviving veterans are still suffering deep wounds from that war.

Even now, one sometimes comes across veterans who are unable to return to normal social life due to psychological scars. It was the Vietnam War that made Americans realize for the first time that their values were not necessarily shared by the rest of the world. In the anti-war movement within the states, even those people who had believed in the USA as a world leader protested against their government about its intervention in another country's affairs.

After the Vietnam War, the US government became much more cautious about involvement in world conflicts and changed its diplomatic policy considerably. American public opinion itself changed, as many became suspicious of the federal government and others simply grew less interested in politics.

USA Public Opinion and the American Disposition

Q: Who were the most popular presidents in America?

The four most popular presidents in America are George Washington (years of office: 1789–1797), the hero of the War of Independence; Abraham Lincoln (Republican, 1861–1865), who liberated slaves and fought the Civil War; Theodore Roosevelt (Republican, 1901–1909), who established the foundation of America today in both domestic and international spheres; and John F. Kennedy (Democrat, 1960–1963), who weathered the Cuban Crisis and approved civil rights.

Americans also favor Franklin Delano Roosevelt (Democrat 1933–45), who rebuilt the American economy after the Great Depression and led the country in WWII; Harry S. Truman (Democrat, 1945–1953), who succeeded President Roosevelt, ended WWII, and had a leading hand in creating the world order after the war; and Ronald Reagan (Republican 1981–1989) who restored the self-confidence of Americans suffering from loss of pride after the Vietnam War and the recession.

From top to bottom: George Washington, Abraham Lincoln, Theodore Roosevelt, John F. Kennedy.

Q: How has the Americans' view of the Japanese changed?

Japan first became widely known in the USA after Commodore Perry brought an end to the country's

Chapter 2 History and Background of the USA

seclusion. For a while the only image in the minds of most Americans was a vague one, that of a somewhat mysterious Oriental people.

Later, as Japanese immigrants came and settled in Hawaii and the West Coast, prejudice and discrimination against them became rampant, mainly originating in disputes over jobs. At the diplomatic level, Japan and the USA had amicable relations until the Japanese-Russo War. After that, however, the two countries became antagonistic due to conflicts in their interests in Asia. This was one factor that eventually led to their clash in WWII.

During WWII, most Japanese-Americans were sent to relocation camps, something for which the US government has recently offered an official apology—acknowledging discrimination and giving compensation to those who underwent such treatment by their own country.

After WWII, Americans' views of the Japanese changed dramatically. The number of Americans who visited Japan after the war and reacted favorably increased. As the Japanese economy recovered, exchanges on a civilian level began to take place.

However, in the 1980s, as the Japanese economy swelled, and full-scale exchange with the USA started, outbreaks of trade and cultural friction occurred.

Nowadays, most Americans and Japanese seem to

think of their countries as having friendly relations, despite some differences that each finds difficult to understand. The recent economic boom in other Asian countries has drawn Americans' attention away from Japan alone, and led to a new appraisal of Japan as just one of America's trading partners within Asia.

Q: What is the most important American value?

The most important value nurtured by Americans is probably "individualism"—a strong belief in oneself and the determination to achieve something through one's own actions.

Other important values might include "independence" and "freedom," which are equally valued by many people.

Yet another important American value is "optimism"—looking toward the future, accepting change, and always trying new things.

Interestingly, neither "individualism" nor "optimism" hold quite such positive value for the Japanese. That difference between Americans and Japanese is probably based on their different cultural backgrounds.

Chapter 3

American Politics

American Democracy

Q: What is the relationship between state and federal governments?

America is basically a country where state governments have a lot of power. Each state has its own constitution and laws. It is the federal government's role to execute domestic affairs that cannot be decided on the state level, such as the minting of money, and to decide diplomatic and military affairs. The functions of the US federal government are thus considerably smaller than those of the Japanese government. State governments handle all those matters that are possible to handle under their own jurisdiction—as long as they do not involve matters to do with the US Constitution.

In 1994, due to the deadlock between the Congress and the president at the time, Bill Clinton, Congress could not pass a national budget and federal services were suspended. But the only way in which the public was affected was in the closure of national parks and the suspension of passport issuance. This

CHAPTER 3 AMERICAN POLITICS

demonstrates how distant the federal government is from the lives of the general public.

Despite this, the role of the federal government has become stronger gradually, due to various social changes that have taken place since the Civil War. State governments, once almost like independent countries, have begun to function more as a part of a nation.

The capitol building in Washington, D.C.

The bombing of the Murrah federal government building in Oklahoma City in the winter of 1995 is an extreme example of some people's opposition of the federal government. The accused in this case are members of militia groups that abhor the federal government's interference in the life of the individual.

Throughout the USA, many people are intent on gaining independence from the federal government for their towns and villages.

Q: What is the history behind the Democratic and Republican Parties?

The Democrats and Republicans are the two major parties constituting the American Congress. The Democratic Party, whose mascot is a donkey, was originally a party opposed to strong government and for regional rights. The Republican Party, whose mascot is an elephant, originally supported strong government after the War of Independence and promoted emancipation of slaves under President Lincoln.

In the twentieth century, this structure was reversed. With the rise of American capitalism, the Republican Party began to protect corporate benefits in keeping with their support of free competition. Conversely, the Democratic Party supported government control over the economy in order to restrain excess capitalism and collaborated with labor unions.

The Democratic Party has continued to make a case for strong government, especially after the Great Depression. They were the party, after all, that revived the American economy through government planning at this time.

The Republican Party, on the other hand, promulgated traditionally American values, supporting free competition and small government. Such policy disagreements emerged symbolically in the confrontation between the Clinton administration and the Republican Party who held a the majority in Congress during the 1990s.

Both parties are enormous. Also, because of the long history behind them, their members have diversified backgrounds, and this sometimes makes a unified position difficult. There are some people who would like to find another way of doing politics—they consider the two existing parties to be stagnant. Ross Perot, who ran in two presidential elections in the 1990s, drew much attention for his influence as an independent third party. Ralph Nader, who was a presidential candidate representing the Green Party in the 2000 election has attracted similar attention for third-party politics.

Q: How does the electoral system work?

In the USA, any citizen over eighteen years old has guaranteed voting rights. One characteristic of the American voting system is that voter registration is voluntary.

Various elections take place in the USA—from local community elections to those on a national government level. Two senators for national government are elected from each state with six-year terms. For the House of Representatives, or Congress, there is a quorum in proportion to each state's population, and each representative's term is two years.

The most important election is the presidential election, conducted every four years. This is actually an indirect election in which voters vote for electors who in turn vote for the candidate. The election of members of Congress and governors, conducted every second year after the presidential election, is called an off-year election and is an important indicator in forecasting the political situation.

Q: What is the role of the president of the United States of America?

The president is the national chief of the USA. Not only is he the chief of the government, but he also has a symbolic role as the head of the nation. The president nominates Cabinet members and carries out policies based on his political beliefs. As the highest military commander, he commands the army, navy, marine corps, and air force, and he carries the final decision on war or ceasefires.

As regards Congress, the president has the power to urge members to pass laws, and he can also veto bills that have passed through Congress.

The US president thus has stronger powers than the Japanese prime minister. At the end of his term (if he is not re-elected), he returns to civilian life. It is up to the nation whether to re-elect a president at the end of his four-year term. Despite the strong power with which he is vested, the president therefore has to pay continual attention to public opinion, and take heed of advice from his close associates.

Chapter 3 American Politics

Q: What are the roles of the US president and Congress, and how are they related?

The current US president is a Democrat, but the majority in the US Congress is Republican. Previously, it was common for the presidents to be Republicans with the majority of Congress Democrats. The system of checks and balances provided by the structure of government has thus been ongoing.

This is probably a sound procedure from the viewpoint of the separation of the three powers (which are judicial, legislative, and executive), the major principle of democracy.

There are some people, however, who criticize this way of doing things: they say people who vote for a president from one party vote for the opposite party as the majority party simply out of growing dissatisfaction and irritation when government and Congress cannot seem to take effective measures against social instability and poverty. As the world changes and international politics and economies fluctuate, American voters' political views tend to shift in one direction and then another. Of course, such election returns might also be a reflection of the American dislike of extreme shifts to the right or left, foreseeable in the case of an administration and Congress of the same party.

At all events, a major problem in the relations

between the present president and Congress is the slow rate of progress in passing bills: the president is either using his veto, or Congress is refusing outright to support his policies.

Q: What do people think of the Bush Administration?

The 9/11 terrorist attacks caused America to suddenly become more right wing, and George W. Bush led the country into wars against Afghanistan and Iraq. In Bush's vision, a strong America would use its economic and military power to bring stability to the world. This idea is referred to as "Neoconservatism." Prisoners from the war in Afghanistan were interred at the Guantanamo military base on the island of Cuba, and there is evidence that people were tortured there. This certainly cast a shadow over the legitimacy of the War on Terror.

The world began to wonder whether the Bush Administration was putting priority on international law or America's needs as a superpower.

Criticism of its foreign policy and the economic recession at the end of Bush's term were major reasons for the staunchly conservative Republican Party's loss of popularity. After eight years of George Bush's government, the Republicans were defeated, and Barack Obama's Democratic administration took over.

Chapter 3 American Politics

Q: What brought about the election of Barack Obama?

In 2008, Americans were worried about the war in Iraq, and also about unemployment and economic uncertainty that were caused by the Lehman Shock. In these difficult times, people were demanding fundamental political reforms, and the Democratic Party adopted the word "Change" as its slogan. The Democrats won easily, and Barack Obama was inaugurated as president in 2009. Obama became the first African-American president in the history of America and was also the first person born in Hawaii to be elected to America's highest office. The Obama administration faced the worst economic situation in recent years, a serious unemployment problem, and on top of that, there were the wars in Afghanistan and Iraq, and the budget deficit was also increasing. It was difficult to implement change, and it has been an uphill battle in terms of his support ratings.

However, in 2011, the economy began to show signs of recovery, most troops were withdrawn from Iraq, and Osama Bin Laden, the mastermind behind the 9/11 terrorist attacks was assassinated, which has increased Obama's appeal with voters.

But is the change that America desires really possible? The Obama Administration is in a very difficult political situation.

The Judicial System and Human Rights

Q: What are the characteristics of the US Constitution?

The US Constitution was proposed in 1787 and promulgated the following year. It is composed of many articles stipulating such things as how to run the Congress of a democratic nation, the power of the president, and so forth. Amendments later added to the articles of the Constitution are particularly important.

The first amendments were made in 1791 and included the following additions: No soldier could be quartered in any house without the consent of the owner (Amendment III); every person has the right to organize a well-regulated militia and to bear arms (Amendment II). These amendments were made just after America attained independence from England, to prevent the nation ever falling under the rule of despotism again.

The War of Independence was an unlawful act

Chapter 3 American Politics

from England's point of view, which made Americans extremely sensitive to individual rights in national trials. The following amendments regarding the human rights of criminals were made: excessive bail and excessive fines are prohibited (Amendment VIII); every person who has committed a crime has a right to trial by an impartial jury chosen from a community of his or her peers.

The forefathers of the USA depicted in a scene of the signing of the Constitution.

A further amendment made in 1951, Amendment XXII, prohibits the president from being elected to office more than twice. Various amendments were thus added as issues concerning rights became more complicated over time.

The underlying principles of the US Constitution consist of the protection of fundamental human rights, the balance and separation of powers, and the guarantee of democracy. These principles are based on the spirit of the Declaration of Independence. The ideas behind the affirmation "that all men are created equal, that they are endowed by their Creator with certain unalienable Rights, that among these are Life, Liberty and the pursuit of Happiness, that to secure these rights, Governments are instituted among Men," became the mainstay of the Constitution. The Amendments were made in order to protect those human rights.

The last part of the Amendments made in 1791 specifies that "The powers not delegated to the United States by the Constitution, nor prohibited by it to the States, are reserved to the States respectively, or to the people." (Amendment X). This Article strongly guarantees the individual freedom and the autonomy of state governments.

Q: What are "civil rights"?

Civil rights are the rights that all people living in the USA are given equally as citizens. In the Declaration of Independence, there is a phrase that "all men are created equal." The question of who these "men" are embodies the history of American civil rights. At the time of the American Revolution, only white men who owned property were guaranteed equality. Slaves were liberated after the Civil War, and later, equal rights for both sexes and the principle of equality for all were established.

Martin Luther King, Jr., was America's most famous advocate for Civil Rights.

The struggle to establish civil rights is called the

civil rights movement. It was most intense from 1955 to the mid-1960s. In 1964, under the direction of the federal government and through the activities of leaders like Martin Luther King, Jr., a law was established to abolish segregation and discrimination on grounds of race, and to protect people from prejudice and violence.

Currently, civil rights laws are enforced strictly, much like the Constitution, as laws that protect the founding principles of the USA. Unfair discrimination not only becomes the subject of civil law suits—very heavy penalties can also be imposed.

Q: What do Americans do to counteract prejudice and discrimination?

The recent widespread changes taking place in official titles symbolizes Americans' sensibility regarding issues of equality.

The "man" of "chairman," for example, refer only to males, so this title has been changed to "chairperson." Similarly, "mailman" has been changed to "mailperson," "Miss" and "Mrs." to "Ms.", and "Oriental" to "Asian" (since the word Oriental evokes a stereotyped image). Such changes are made in Japan too, nowadays, but not as frequently as in the USA.

This movement has recently developed beyond gender and race to cover discrimination against homosexuals.

Affirmative action is something that has accordingly become a subject of much discussion.

Affirmative action is a system established under the law to underpin the principle of equality guaranteed by civil rights laws. It promotes opportunities for minorities to advance in society by providing advantageous conditions for college enrollment, as well as company and public job employment to persons from historically disadvantaged groups or groups that have suffered discrimination.

Under this system, conditions required for college enrollment are moderated or a special employment framework is created for employment. Companies that practice affirmative action are encouraged in various ways—for example, they can be given preferential treatment from federal and state government when orders are placed.

Affirmative action laws are sometimes criticized as contradicting the principle of equal opportunity and creating reverse discrimination. The Republican governor of California, Pete Wilson, abolished affirmative action in that state in 1996. Again in 2010, the California Supreme Court upheld the ban.

A controversy as to what true equality is surrounds the issue of affirmative action.

Chapter 3 American Politics

Q: What are the characteristics of the US trial system?

In the USA most judgments are made based on jury verdict. The jury delivers a verdict of guilty or not guilty, and the judge gives a judgment accordingly. This system is based on the British tradition but maintained with a very American sense of doing justice to the will of the community. A closer look shows that provisions for the trial system, prosecution, and judgment differ from state to state. Finance-related cases, crimes affecting a wide area, and criminal cases involving the federal government are tried in federal court.

First, the defendant accepts the Grand Jury verdict of whether or not he or she is to be tried at court. The jury then tries the case accordingly with legal advice from the court, and brings in a verdict of guilty or not guilty.

The jury is selected by the court using voting lists and other means. Citizens are obliged by law to do jury duty. If a juror is obviously biased for or against the defendant, the lawyer can plead that he or she be dismissed. Such bargaining is an important part of trial process.

During the trial, the defense and prosecution lawyers conduct a fight with words. The two sides defend and prosecute the defendant, and try to persuade the jury their way. In America, if a defendant is judged not guilty, prosecutors cannot appeal, and this causes both sides to put up a furious fight.

Q: What is legal bargaining in the USA?

Legal bargaining involves the reduction of penalties for cooperation in criminal investigations, or cooperation with prosecutors by confessing the crime. This is not a system per se, and no guarantee exists that the defendant will receive an advantageous judgment even if he or she cooperates with the prosecution.

In cases where a crime is spread out over a wide area, like organized crime activity, cooperation from the defendant leads to the prosecution of other major criminals. In such a case, the prosecution pleads for extenuating circumstances to be considered in court.

There are many cases of legal bargaining. In one trial in which a New York mafia boss was sentenced to life imprisonment, a murderer who had cooperated with the investigation was released after only a short incarceration.

Q: Is there capital punishment in the USA?

Some states permit capital punishment, and others do not. As of 2011, there are sixteen states without capital punishment, including Washington, D.C. Many US trust territories such as Guam or Puerto Rico have also abolished the death penalty.

The rights or wrongs of the death penalty are always a major theme in political debates in the USA, where some atrocious crimes are committed. Capital punishment also applies to criminals tried under federal law (crimes against federal government facilities or financial organizations, crimes carried out over a wide area, etc.).

The number of prisoners on death row in 2010 totaled 3,267.

Domestic Affairs

Q: What is the size, total revenue, and expenditure of the current US federal budget?

The US government has put various policies into effect in an attempt to reduce the chronic budget deficit. In the process of balancing expenditures and revenues over the past several years, the president and Congress have not always seen eye to eye. Frequent arguements arise over what should be reduced in the budget, and how to put programs into effect.

Although Congressional Republicans opposed the plan, the Obama administration passed a policy for federal healthcare in 2010. The administration also enacted a "stimulus" plan to help the nation recover from the economic crash of 2008. As a result of these heavy federal expenditures, Republicans in Congress have devoted much of the duration of the Obama presidency to "cut federal spending."

In the 2011 federal budget, total revenue was estimated at $2.17 trillion and total estimated expenditures were $3.82 trillion, with a $1.65 trillion deficit. The deficit has been increasing since 2001 when George W. Bush took over from the Clinton administration. The current federal deficit holds a record high.

Q: What kind of police system exists in the USA?

A separate police force exists in each and every state, and the force acts in accordance with that state's laws. The FBI (the Federal Bureau of Investigation—in essence, the federal police), acts above and beyond regional boundaries in the investigation of widespread crimes, finance-related crimes, and crimes against the federal government. The FBI also cooperates with local police in their investigations. Other federal organizations, such as the DEA (Drug Enforcement Administration), play their own part in the investigation of widespread drug crimes.

Q: What are the characteristics of the American tax system?

April 15th is the last date for taxpayers to file tax returns for the previous year's income. In the USA, company workers have to file income taxes even if tax has been withdrawn at the source. There are three kinds of forms to file: city, state, and federal.

As filing day draws near, people consider how they can pay fewer taxes, and they get the advice of accountants as they fill out their return forms. They try to work out how they can make personal expenses business expenses, or whether they might be exempt from paying local taxes since they were away on business trips.

Taxes are divided into direct taxes and indirect taxes, just as in Japan. Indirect taxes differ considerably from state to state. For example, the sales tax (an indirect tax) of New York City is 8.875%, while New Jersey's is 7%—so some people from New York drive to this neighboring state for their large purchases.

Q: How does the US educational system differ from the Japanese system?

The biggest difference between the US and Japanese educational systems is that most US education is administered by state. The local community plays a major role in deciding the school curriculum, textbooks, teaching materials, and the budget, which are not allocated at a set national average. The parents of children who attend schools and residents of the city or state have a bigger say over local education than the federal government.

The content and quality of education therefore vary from region to region. The education children receive also varies according to the type of community they belong to. For example, in some Christian communities, Darwin's theory of evolution is not taught in social studies or biology. Wealthier parents sometimes move to regions with better schools, or send their children to private school.

One strength of the US educational system is that people can participate actively in deciding the education they want for their children rather than simply accepting a curriculum that has been decided for them by the government. Children generally start attending school at the age of six, though this varies by region. The school year begins in September (in some regions, in October). As in Japan, children attend elementary, junior high, and high schools for twelve years, and then some go on to college. Usually, they attend school for twelve years, but again, this number varies.

Welfare and Health

Q: What is the major cause of death among Americans?

According to statistics, the overwhelming cause of death among Americans is heart disease. The second cause is cancer, and next is car accidents. Average life expectancy is 76 years; the infant mortality rate is 6.7 out of 1,000.

Health problems among socially disadvantaged groups, low-income people, or new immigrants are a source of concern. The infant mortality rate of non-white minorities is fifteen times higher than that among the white population. Tuberculosis and AIDS are also spreading among minority groups. One challenge America faces is how to solve the economic-based issues of race and health.

Q: What kind of health insurance system does the USA have?

As of 2011, almost 17 percent of Americans are reported not to be covered by health insurance. That is because no national health insurance system exists in the USA. Most people are covered by the insurance that their employer or they themselves buy. However, this is costly for people who are unemployed, or for non-contractual workers such as part-timers. Moreover, for those who have experienced past illnesses or medical conditions, insurance premiums are quite high. The fact is that many people simply cannot afford health insurance.

However, sweeping health care reforms were proposed and passed by the Obama administration in 2010. These reforms mandate all US citizens to have health insurance, while also enacting regulations to keep the cost of health insurance down.

National systems in which the federal government covers medical expenses do exist, such as Medicaid for seniors and Medicare for low-income people. With the federal deficit increasing, however, there is some question as to whether these systems will continue in their present form.

American Diplomacy

Q: What is US isolationism?

As the War of Independence and subsequent historical developments demonstrate, the USA was a nation created by people who united in a common desire to be free of the tyranny of European governments.

Not surprisingly, US public opinion shows great opposition to any national intervention in the affairs of foreign countries. America became an independent nation only by their own great efforts, one step at a time, and as a result there is a perception that America should keep well away from European disputes. This idea runs through their policies of non-alliance.

President Monroe emphasized a policy of isolationism in 1817. It was later called the Monroe Doctrine after him.

The USA officially abandoned isolationism after the Japanese attacked Pearl Harbor. Until then, the USA had been sympathetic to England and France in World War II, but the USA had remained on the sidelines. The Japanese attack brought the USA rushing into war, and thereafter it took a leading role in the international arena.

A certain tradition of isolationism still remains however. The failure of the Vietnam War impressed upon the American public the stupidity of overseas intervention, and voices were heard in Congress arguing that the country should maintain its distance from other countries to "keep America great."

Isolationism is not simply a diplomatic policy: it is also an expression of a certain type of generalized nationalism that reaches down to the general public. This is a nationalism that believes in the protection of America as a nation.

Q: In what ways did US diplomacy change after the end of the Cold War?

With the end of the Cold War, the USA lost its more powerful rival, the Soviet Union. But in fact as a result the world has become an even more complicated place, and the possibility of regional disputes only the more likely. This seems to be the view of most people in the American government. Current US diplomatic policy, therefore,

Ronald Reagan and Mikhail Gorbachev meet during Cold War talks.

seems to consist of taking a leading role in global stabilization: for example, the USA helped bring about peace talks in the Mideast, and has made positive efforts toward stabilizing the situation in Russia.

The biggest issue that concerns American policy in Asia is how the USA will pursue its relations with China. Other international issues that the USA deals with are problems arising from economic development in various countries in Southeast Asia, and the stability of the Korean Peninsula.

Q: What is "human rights diplomacy"?

Human rights diplomacy became the principle axis of US diplomacy under President Carter. The key idea is that the USA, a nation with democracy as a national policy, applies economic sanctions or diplomatic pressure to any nation violating human rights. This is done in order to defend democracy and to promote global stability. Admittedly, behind such diplomacy lay a US intention to curb the power of the Soviet Union during the Cold War, and to justify and publicize America's power after the Cold War.

Actually, American human rights diplomacy became a political rallying point for all sorts of people suffering unjust discrimination and oppression around the world. It has shown demonstrable results.

But such diplomacy can be taken as "meddlesome," and sometimes the other country simply becomes more stubborn and relations grow worse. The awkward relations the USA had with China after the Tiananmen Square massacre is one such example.

Human rights diplomacy supports an American ideal. But the world is diverse, and it is getting more so. Many different views exist about the issue of human rights alone. It is no longer practically viable for the USA to be the "global policeman" it was during the period after WWII. Moreover, one cannot ignore the contradiction in the American position: even while it advocates human rights abroad, the death penalty exists in most states, and stronger restrictions are being imposed on the number of immigrants fleeing poverty and oppression and entering US borders.

Even though it is underpinned by American ideals and pride, American human rights diplomacy is actually used as a bargaining tool in foreign relations, so it is a policy surrounded by much controversy.

Q: What is the relationship of the USA with the UN?

Together with England and the Soviet Union, the USA played a major role in founding the United Nations. The Atlantic Charter announced by British Prime Minister Winston Churchill and American President

Chapter 3 American Politics

Franklin D. Roosevelt in 1941 became the founding spirit of the United Nations. This was developed into the UN Charter at the UN Conference in San Francisco in 1945.

When the UN was established, the USA became a permanent member, along with France, England, China (then the "Republic of China"), and the Soviet Union. As the Cold War advanced, the USA took the initiative as a representative of the interest of free nations in using the UN as an important negotiation arena in international politics.

With the end of the Cold War, the whole purpose and existence of the UN, which after all was founded in the aftermath of WWII, has come into question. The USA is no longer concerned first and foremost with how to deal with the Communist bloc: it is now attempting to figure out how to further US interests in the UN given the more complicated international situation.

Q: How has US diplomacy with Japan changed?

After WWII, the key point of US diplomacy with Japan was how best to incorporate Japan into the group of free nations. The USA concluded the US-Japan Security Treaty, helped build the Japanese economy after the devastation of war and set Japan up as a strategic point in the Far East.

As Japan achieved high economic growth and prospered, however, the Japanese economy became a threat. As a result, the USA made drastic changes in its diplomatic policy toward Japan. They tried to remove various unfair elements previously overlooked in the two countries' economies. The USA also began to ask Japan to take responsibility in the area of the military, in proportion to its economic power.

The post-war era is now over, and so is the Cold War. US diplomacy with Japan seems to have entered a new phase. Though the North Korean issue remains unresolved, and the threat from China still exists, the USA is working toward improving relations with China, which will be an important player in twenty-first-century diplomacy.

Under such circumstances, heaps of questions surround Japan's relationship with the USA. Will it be possible for the two countries to cooperate as major partners working to ensure global stability? Or will Japan have to confront the USA as a rival? Most likely both these things will occur.

Q: What effect did 9/11 have on America?

On September 11, 2001, hijacked civilian aircraft crashed into the World Trade Center in New York and the Pentagon, the Department of Defense's building on the outskirts of Washington, D.C. Nearly 3,000 people were killed in the attack.

The two World Trade Center towers right after the terrorist attack of 9/11.

This incident was a turning point in American history. First of all, it was a lesson in how defenseless America is to terrorism. After the attack, all the airports and important institutions in America had to tighten their security measures.

In addition, public opinion moved to the right, and the American public began to hate and fear the radical Islamic sect that the terrorists belonged to. This hate and fear became discrimination toward all believers in Islam, and threatened the democratic acceptance of diversity that America had promoted for many years. At the same time, the Bush Administration declared the "War on Terror" and began to take action against anti-American organizations and governments around the world. Afghanistan was invaded because it supported terrorist groups, and the Taliban regime, which controlled it, was destroyed.

Furthermore, America decided to invade Iraq and destroy the regime of Saddam Hussein because of its support for anti-American groups.

These actions created a backlash against America, and the anti-terrorist measures awoke hatred in the hearts of many Muslims. Throughout the world, and in the Middle East in particular, this situation caused great tension.

The World Trade Center was a symbol not just of New York, but of America itself. The image of the destruction of these two soaring towers was so shocking that after the attacks, the media refrained from showing certain scenes of their destruction. Many people say that America's democratic virtue of freely accepting diverse cultures was destroyed along with the World Trade Center.

There is a belief in America that democratic freedom should be spread around the world. This belief became much stronger after 9/11.

America requested military aid from its allies abroad, including Japan. A new military order was established in the name of fighting terrorism, and Japan was thrust into joining it.

From that perspective, 9/11 was an event that had an important influence not just on America, but on the world as well.

Q: How do people feel about the assassination of Osama Bin Laden?

For almost a decade after 9/11, America searched for Osama Bin Laden, the leader of the organization that carried out the worst terrorist attacks in US history.

In May of 2011, when Bin Laden was assassinated at

Chapter 3 American Politics

the compound where he was hiding in Pakistan, Americans celebrated it as a great victory in the War on Terror.

However, it is a fact that this action has created new resentment of America, and there are fears that it may trigger further terrorism. Moreover, the United States sent troops into the sovereign nation of Pakistan without permission from the government. Some people have called this an act of war, and Bin Laden did not receive a trial. Many question whether these actions are acceptable for a democratic country to carry out, and there is debate about whether this sort of thing can be permitted under international law.

Osama Bin Laden was assassinated on May 2, 2011.

Bin Laden's relatives are some of the most powerful people in Saudi Arabia and have many connections in American economic circles. In addition, Osama Bin Laden and other Muslim believers received direct support from the American government during the war against the Soviet Union.

There is a long history of both discord and cooperation between America and fundamentalist Islam, and Osama Bin Laden was a symbol of that complicated relationship.

Ever since the foundation of the state of Israel in 1948, it has been supported by the US, and there have been confrontations with the expelled Palestinians. For the US, the Middle East is the most sensitive area in the world, and America's use of military diplomacy there is a very difficult issue.

What influence the assassination of Bin Laden will have on this situation is a matter of great concern.

American Military and Space Development

Q: Does the USA still place an emphasis on the military?

In the 1990s, as a part of the deficit reduction, the federal government made efforts to reduce military expenditures. The government closed down military bases in the US. Military spending was $303.6 billion in 1989, but it was reduced to $271.9 billion in 1995. However, in the twenty-first century, military spending is back on the rise. In 2010, the US government spent $663.8 billion on the Department of Defense, military research and development, and overseas operations.

The consciousness of the USA's leadership role in global stability is strongly alive. However, with a staggering federal deficit, the government is struggling with the issue of maintaining American presence while also making cuts in military expenditure. The USA is restricting its contribution to the UN PKO, so it looks as if diplomatic rather than military strategy will emerge as the most important feature of its international politics.

Q: How is the CIA thought of in the USA?

In May 1994, federal prosecutors accused CIA agent Aldrich H. Ames of having sold state secrets to the Soviet Union over a period of nine years. The information he sold was highly important, including a list of Soviet and Eastern European spies working for the USA. The espionage network on the US side was left in ruins. On the Soviet side, at least ten spies selling information to the USA were reportedly executed.

The official seal of the Central Intelligence Agency (CIA).

In the midst of this scandal, the CIA was unable to prepare itself for a very important development in world affairs—the collapse of the Soviet Union and the end of the Cold War.

Those incidents fostered suspicion about the whole

purpose and existence of the CIA, and a debate was held in Congress as to whether the CIA was still relevant to the modern world. The CIA argues that the world is not yet stable, so there was still a reason for its being. Although the CIA itself denies them, there are reports that the USA has started economic espionage on its rivals, including Japan, to ensure its survival.

Q: What is the future of US space development?

Currently, the US government sets a strict ceiling on the space development budget in its commitment to reduce the national budget. The 2010 budget for NASA was $18.7 billion. But NASA is still managing to promote space development. They are developing a new heavy lift rocket program, and it is retrofitting its space centers to reflect new, modern technologies.

As far as development is concerned, NASA is concentrating its efforts on probing the solar system, particularly Mars. It is possible that human beings might journey to Mars in the twenty-first century. In 2010, a US bill was signed allowing for a manned Mars mission by the 2030s. NASA is also constructing a space station with Russia, Europe, and Japan as a base for space development, hoping to complete it by the year 2012.

Chapter 4

The US Economy

Background of the US Economy

Q: What kind of currency is the US dollar?

In the same way as the Japanese yen is officially referred to as a Bank of Japan note, the US dollar is officially called a Federal Reserve note—and it is issued and controlled by the Federal Reserve Bank. It was actually in 1913 that the central bank of the US began to issue and control currency and standardize its finance policies. Previous to that, banks were left almost entirely to their own devices under a decentralized system. The frontier was apparently overrun by financial institutions (nicknamed "wildcat banks") making chaotic credit transactions, issuing bank notes of their own and causing frequent financial crises.

US dollars are now distributed in six kinds of bills, in denominations from 1 to 100 dollars, with supplementary coins—1 cent (a penny), 5 cents (a nickel), 10 cents (a dime), 25 cents (a quarter), 50 cents (a half dollar) and 1 dollar. The slang name for a dollar is a "buck." Thus one often hears 2 dollars expressed as "2 bucks" in daily life.

Q: When did the US dollar begin to have international distribution?

The huge safes underneath the New York Federal Reserve Bank store gold belonging to every country. Whenever a debt is paid by one country to another, the gold moves from one safe to another underground.

The Federal Reserve Bank is now a tourist spot too, a reminder of the time gold flowed into the USA based on the high value accorded the US dollar.

The US dollar became the key world currency when the USA became the world's largest creditor after WWII. In the latter half of the 1960s, however, the US economy declined, and the dollar was seen to have less value than before—and it was in fact devalued. World currency then shifted to a floating standard.

The US dollar is still a key world currency, but it is no longer the standard of all exchange and value. World currencies all affect each other in the current dynamic world markets, which is a source of mixed blessings as far as the US financial and business worlds are concerned.

Q: What regional differences exist in the US domestic economy?

Considerable differences in terms of income, wage, and economic power exist from state to state in the USA. No single center like Tokyo exists, and since most large enterprises develop where they were founded, companies tend to be scattered all over the country. Procter & Gamble, for example, a huge manufacturer of household goods and necessities, has its headquarters in Cincinnati, Ohio. Detroit and its environs have a large concentration of car manufacturers, and Coca-Cola's headquarters are in Atlanta. But generally speaking, financial business and the media are concentrated in New York, manufacturers and distributors in the Midwest, and the high-tech industry on the West Coast.

Q: What shifts have there been in the US trade balance?

The US has been troubled by a trade deficit for many years now. Recently, the deficit is most outstanding with China, Mexico, Japan, and Germany. The US trade balance turned to deficit in the 1980s—particularly the mid-'80s, when it exceeded $95 billion. This was exacerbated by the decline of the auto industry, which brought serious trade friction with Japan. But the deficit is recently declining. According to

Chapter 4 The US Economy

Department of Commerce statistics, the 2011 deficit was $48.2 billion.

Opinions vary about how to interpret these statistics. One opinion even has it that the US trade deficit, particularly that with Japan, is actually a surplus if one takes into consideration wire transaction, the money people bring into the US on their persons, the money Japanese companies in the US invest, and the revenues they attain from export.

Q: What items does the US export and import?

Major US export items include computer telecommunication apparatuses, airplanes and related parts, cars, machine tools, scientific equipment, chemicals and agricultural products. Major import items include cars, industrial products, computer telecommunication apparatuses, machine tools, steel and metal products, paper, chemical products, clothing and petroleum products. The US thus imports many of the same sort of items as it exports. The fact that it imports materials to produce goods to be exported shows how bound up with the world economy the US economy is.

The fact that the US exports and imports both materials and products rather than just manufactured goods—which is the general pattern of advanced

Q: What is the Lehman Shock?

Lehman Brothers was one of America's most famous investment banks. When it went bankrupt in 2008, it affected financial markets around the world at a time when there was a world-wide recession.

In 2007, housing loans for low-income earners called "subprime loans" caused the amount of bad debt held by banks to increase, and there was an economic crisis similar to the bursting of Japan's economic bubble in the early 90s.

Lehman Brothers lost huge amounts of money because of all its bad debt resulting from subprime loans, and it went bankrupt.

This caused a panic that lasted almost two years, and things like the collapse of the Greek economy have created even more instability and strengthened the Lehman Shock's effect.

From the crash in stock prices after 9/11 to the collapse

The headquarters of Lehman Brothers in Times Square.

Chapter 4 The US Economy

of the IT bubble to the Lehman Shock, the world's leading economy has had a very bumpy ride. The world is watching to see if America will be able to overcome the challenges it faces and recover.

Q: What will the future of environment-related businesses be?

When President Obama took office in the wake of the Lehman Shock, one of his important promises was to give support to environment-related businesses. One of his main tasks was restoring demand for automobiles during a recession which brought about the bankruptcy of the world's largest automaker, General Motors. Soon after, the important Japanese automaker Toyota began to struggle due to a recall scandal and production problems related to the 2011 Tohoku Earthquake. How the American car industry will respond to this situation is not yet clear. Japanese technology for producing eco-friendly cars is said to be more advanced than that of other countries, but how will the American car industry respond? Many questions remain.

It is very important to be able to predict how America will be able to compete in terms of green technology, energy, and production, and this ability will have a big impact on how well it can compete globally, now and in the future. Until now, America has been a materialistic society and the world's economic superpower. Dealing with global warming and other environmental problems that are presenting new economic challenges will be an important political issue that must be dealt with. In the future, how environment-related businesses can predict the future of the giant American market and compete with competitors such as Japan will affect America's economic growth.

US Industries

Q: What is the current situation of the US auto industry?

In the 1980s, the US auto industry declined, and many lay-offs occurred, as pressure was felt from the auto industry in Japan and Germany. The general opinion of American cars was that they had poor fuel efficiency and were continually breaking down.

The auto industry is a key one, a lifeline to all sorts of other industries. Its stagnation had a ripple effect all

Chapter 4 The US Economy

over the US industrial world. But the US auto industry made a wonderful comeback in the 1990s. Ford, for example, had great success with its pickup trucks and Taurus family cars, and in 1996 sold nearly 3.3 million cars. This boom posed a threat to Japanese auto manufacturers like Honda that had made such inroads in the US markets.

GM headquarters.

However, these days foreign cars are once again catching up, and the US auto industry has been crippled by the economic crash of 2008. Rising oil costs and a new consumer awareness of carbon footprints also contributed to the sharp decline of US car manufacturing. The "Big Three" of the US automotive industry—Ford, General Motors, and Chrysler—had to request $25 billion in federal assistance to stay afloat in 2008. The federal government loaned them $17.4 billion. Currently, China tops the list of global leaders in auto manufacturing, with 18.3 million cars produced in 2010. Japan follows with 9.6 million cars produced, and the US trails behind at third place with 7.7 million.

Q: What is the current state of the US computer industry?

In 1981, IBM, a leader of the computer industry,

introduced the personal computer, or PC. Since then, the computer industry has grown tremendously, and has become a dynamo of the US economy.

This industry showed particularly high growth in the 1990s with the proliferation of the Internet and PCs. There was also an increased demand for PCs overseas. According to Computer Industry Almanac statistics, 264.1 million personal computers were in use in the US in 2008. This number is expected only to grow.

In 2008, the US computer industry generated $50.6 billion, showing a 3.8 percent annual growth rate.

The computer industry is said to be an industry where individual talent can give rise to huge enterprises and where dreams of success can indeed be realized—there is the famous example of Microsoft Corporation. Indeed one noticeable feature of this industry is the prolific growth of many entrepreneurs.

Apple headquarters in Cupertino, California.

Q: What kind of place is Silicon Valley?

Silicon Valley is the nickname for the area stretching from South San Francisco to San Jose where a great

Chapter 4 The US Economy

many hi-tech companies are concentrated. It is famous not only for its hi-tech industry, but also as a place where the best and the brightest from all over the world have gathered in search of just such an environment. Many Japanese and European companies have also moved into this area, making it a computer-networked global village.

Q: What future trends can be foreseen in the US space industry?

The US aviation industry is collaborating in space development with NASA and others. For example, 36% of the orders for Boeing's non-commercial-flight craft market is for NASA's space program. This is much larger than the Air Force's order. Areas of development include designing economical and efficient spaceships, but attention will also be given to the military use of space, the protection of the earth's environment and other development projects, the application of space development technology to the telecommunications industry, and much else besides. Space-related business looks like it will continue to grow in the twenty-first century.

The space shuttle Columbia launching.

Q: What is the current state of US agriculture?

The agricultural industry in the USA has developed over a vast farmland, in which a single farm can be as much as 160 times larger than one in Japan. Large-scale machinery and advanced technology are used.

Many farmers have made a lot of money by advancing into the manufactured food market. Anthony Rossi, who founded Tropicana Products, the largest American juice producer which is expanding all over the world, immigrated to the US from Italy with only $30 in his pocket. After many hardships, he started a farming business in Florida, then got into the juice industry and founded his huge company.

Despite the sharp decrease in the farming population now, the sheer scale of US agriculture makes it a world leader, surpassing even the Soviet Union.

Agricultural products are an important American export item. Total wheat and corn exports amount to $9.45 billion, the most in the world. Rice exports are second only to Thailand; total meat production is 31.35 million tons, also the most in the world.

But serious problems exist in agriculture: bankruptcy of farms due to excessive investment, and decrease of land for cultivation caused by over-application of fertilizer and drought. The farming population is expected to decrease. US agriculture

Q: What is the current state of America's IT industry?

In the 90s, the IT business, and Silicon Valley in particular, grew into a huge industry that revolutionized people's lives and communications around the world.

In May 2011, the IT industry giant Microsoft bought Skype, a software application that allows users to make voice calls or have video chats over the Internet. This and other investments are having an incredible effect in stimulating this futuristic industry. At the end of the twentieth century, however, speculators were putting too much money into the IT industry, and in the first months of the twenty-first century, the bursting of so-called "dot-com bubble" triggered a financial crisis in America. However, even today, IT is a major industry and has a huge influence on both the everyday lives of Americans and the overall economy.

The IT business is well suited to the pioneering, risk-taking American spirit, and it has also taken in immigrants from around

Silicon Valley stretches from South San Francisco to San Jose, and is home to many hi-tech companies.

the world, resulting in an industry that fosters the talents of the capable people who work in it. It is common knowledge that among the leaders in the IT industry, a great number come from India and other Asian countries.

Companies such as the on-line shopping giant Amazon, the industry-leading search engine Google, and the famous competitors Microsoft and Apple were all created in America, and these businesses have expanded all over the world. They are the new foundations of America's economy.

American Management and Office Environments

Q: What does sexual harassment refer to in the USA?

It is quite common in America for sexual harassment to become the subject of court cases. It is not only a question of whether someone sexually harasses another person. For example, someone in the office

CHAPTER 4 THE US ECONOMY

may download a nude pin-up from a men's magazine into his computer. A woman who witnesses this can file a protest with the company, claiming that such behavior shows contempt for women and makes the office environment uncomfortable. If the company ignores her protest, she can take legal action, claiming an irresponsible attitude on the part of the company.

Sexual harassment in the US is thus an issue considered in reference to laws stipulating sexual equality at the workplace designed to counter situations that make the workplace uncomfortable for reasons related to sex.

Q: What is equal opportunity in corporate management?

One of the issues American corporate management has to pay a great deal of attention to is observation of the equal opportunity law. This civil rights law stipulates that no one should suffer discrimination nor discomfort in the workplace on grounds of race, gender, religion, physical disability, or country of origin. Some states also prohibit discrimination against homosexuality and other private sexual matters, as well as age.

The law was established with its main premise as equal treatment for all. It has strong binding powers that essentially oblige management to abolish all discrimination in the workplace to create a pleasant working environment. Employees do not hesitate to raise complaints about their boss, or even company owners, if any problem arises under the law or the spirit of the law. Corporate equality is thus something about which management exercises a lot of thought.

Q: What are American working hours?

It is a bit of a cliche to imagine that Americans leave the office as soon as 5:00 p.m. comes around. Some people work long hours and think nothing of coming to the office on weekends if necessary. The workdays of people in venture businesses in urban areas are very long indeed. Large corporations, however, have strictly fixed working hours in accordance with union regulations.

Generally, working hours are considered a matter of individual responsibility, just as long as the allocated task gets done. No custom exists in the US for staying after-hours in order to develop relationships with colleagues or participate in group activities, as in Japan. In the USA people believe that the hours after work should be spent on one's personal life.

Chapter 4 The US Economy

Q: What is the wage standard in the US?

According to 2010 statistics, the annual average income per person in the US is $46,326. The wage differential, however, is very great, and it is not unusual for the difference between management and the more general worker to be as much as $1 million. Since it is a principle of American equality that anybody with talent can succeed and become rich, it is highly unlikely that the wage differential will disappear.

There is also a big difference in wage standard according to region. The differential between Mississippi, the state with the lowest average income, and New Hampshire, with the highest, amounts to $30,000. Wealth disparity is increasing in the US, and it has become a social problem. Gender equality has been established by law, but the average income of a woman with a master's degree is roughly 70% of that of a man with the same education. The wage differential is currently an important equality issue.

Q: What are some characteristics of the way Americans run businesses?

The most notable characteristic of American business practice is probably the way people are employed on the basis of capability. Once they are employed, evaluation is made solely on their achievement. Also, every respect is given to employees' freedom and independence.

Of course, superiors must point out areas where improvement can be made when the time for evaluation comes around, but the method is left up to the employee's discretion.

Japanese companies use a method of employing recent graduates and educating them over time in the job. In the US, companies do not nurture employees in the same way. Companies provide the opportunity for growth, but fostering one's abilities and career is always left up to individual responsibility. If necessary, employees can ask for certain education opportunities to be provided by the company.

So when employees do not live up to their contract, or if they are dissatisfied with their jobs or treatment, both sides can renegotiate the contract, and sometimes the contract is simply broken by one side.

Chapter 5

Society—Life

The American Living Environment

Q: What is the relationship between upper-middle class and low-income families?

America is a country based on the principle of equality, so no social system of class exists. Recently, however, a significant disparity has arisen in wealth and educational background, and divisions between social strata are definitely noticeable.

The relationship between the upper-middle class and low-income families is often cited as an example of the difference between social strata.

Americans often say that their society is polarized into two groups. There are the upper-middle classes, which are those who live affluently, particularly in urban areas, and the low-income families, who live in slum sections of the same urban areas. This distinct division is becoming a major social problem. Children born into the poor segments of the population suffer disadvantages in terms of education. Insufficient school facilities exist due to these communities' lack of financial resources. Children without a chance of an adequate education hang around in the streets, get caught up in crimes and drugs, and these communities become even more alienated from others than before.

The conflict between the "haves" and the "have-nots" grows more serious day by day. The most important issue to be dealt with in the US is how to stop this vicious cycle—how to solve the problem of education and how to prevent the cities' slide into urban decay.

Q: Do gay people receive equal treatment in the US?

It was in the late 1960s that gay rights came to the forefront. The idea that no one should be discriminated against because of their sexuality developed into a kind of civil rights movement. Gay rights campaigners lobbied that job rejection, dismissal, or harassment based on homosexuality was a violation of human rights. Equal opportunities without discrimination for jobs and promotion in government was guaranteed in 1975. Discrimination against gays is gradually being wiped out.

In recent years, homosexual people have come into considerable protection under the law. Discrimination at job sites is illegal, and employers will be punished if it is seen to exist. The issue of whether gays should be accepted in the military has been the subject of much debate. In the 1990s, a "Don't Ask, Don't Tell" policy was adopted, in which recruiters do not inquire about sexuality in recruitment interviews. However, this policy is now pending repeal in the federal government.

Another recent issue has been whether to legally recognize gay marriages. Currently, gay marriage is not recognized legally in most American states, but the issue is likely to undergo much attention in the future.

Q: Which cities and areas in the US are the most popular?

The most popular places to live for Americans are Seattle, with its mild climate close to the mountains and ocean, Aspen and other Colorado towns in the bosom of the Rockies, West Palm Beach and other cities in Florida, which are great retirement places, San Francisco, with its mild climate and beautiful scenery, and the New England state of Vermont, which is close to Canada and

Downtown Aspen, Colorado. Aspen is famous for its mountain scenery and ideal skiing conditions.

a perfect place to get away from the bustle of East Coast cities.

Recent reports say that people living in big cities like Los Angeles and New York are moving out to the countryside to live. Here, they can telecommute via Internet, and when occasion demands they go into their workplace from the local airports. These people seem to be the precursors of an exodus from the cities.

Religion

Q: What are the characteristics of religion in the USA?

It was the Protestants who first came across the ocean in search of a free, new world and settled in America. Later, many more Protestants emigrated from various parts of Europe, and their influence is still strong in the US today.

In certain regions of the Mid-West, such as Missouri or Kansas, the Protestant Church still has a great influence. This area is often called the "Bible Belt."

In the nineteenth century, a great number of Catholic immigrants came from Ireland, Italy, and other countries. There are now as many as 68 million Catholics in the US.

Recently the younger generations hold religion in a kind of suspicion, and fewer people are attending church. There has been an increase in religions new to North America, such as Buddhism, Islam, etc., especially in urban areas. Many black people in particular have become Muslims, identifying with their places of origin.

But as we see from such ceremonies as the Presidential Inauguration, where the president puts his hand on the Bible to take the oath, the influence of Christianity in the US is still strong.

Q: What kind of religion is Protestantism?

Protestantism is the religion Martin Luther started in Germany in the sixteenth century, in opposition to Catholicism. It was designated as heresy by the Vatican, which had tremendous power, and its followers were persecuted. But many kings in Europe who wanted to escape the Vatican's influence gave it support. A long period of upheaval in Europe followed when the continent was divided between the two religions. Various sects of Protestantism scattered all

Chapter 5 Society—Life

over Europe and further complicated the situation.

It was these Protestants who had suffered persecution and exile that set sail for the New World. For them, the great continent was virgin territory—here, they thought, was the "promised land," given to them by God.

Protestant people have a strong work ethic—labor is part of their creed. They worked diligently in the new land, carrying out development projects and starting various businesses. Protestant beliefs and the values nurtured by them were an important fuel that helped America come about.

Q: What is the Mormon Church?

The Mormon religion was founded by Joseph Smith in 1830 in the northern part of New York. It is thus a religion born in America. Its official name is the Church of Jesus Christ of Latter-day Saints.

Mormon doctrine holds that God, Jesus Christ, and many of the saints walked on American soil in ancient times. The Book of Mormon, given by God, is its sacred book. The Mormon religion preaches that the land of God will be established in the New World.

Mormons were persecuted in many places because of the religion's unique doctrine and its acceptance of polygamy. Many Mormons moved to Ohio, or Illinois, and eventually, in 1847, found a place to settle in Salt Lake City, Utah.

The system of polygamy was abandoned at the end of the nineteenth century, with encouragement from the federal government. Mormons are enthusiastic evangelists. They dispatch many missionaries to Japan. Mormon believers total 4.6 million in the US, and 70% of the Utah population is said to be Mormon.

Q: What kind of base does Catholicism have in the USA?

Catholicism began to increase around the mid-nineteenth century, with the great influx of immigrants from Ireland and Italy. Before that time, most immigrants were Protestants.

Recent Catholic immigrants have come from Mexico, the Caribbean, and other Latin American countries, areas that previously were under the influence of Spain. Catholics total 68 million. Presidents Kennedy and Reagan were both Catholic.

Q: Are there religious conflicts in the USA?

Although religious conflict was not as intense as in Europe, historically, religious suppression has occurred in the US, as has friction between religions. But after the promulgation of the Constitution,

Chapter 5 Society—Life

which extolled freedom of religion, such occurrences became less frequent. Doctrinal differences, and differences concerning ethics, however, do give rise to serious confrontations. The most significant example surrounds the issue of abortion. The anti-abortionists claim that abortion is murder, while the pro-abortionists think that the matter should be left up to the individual, without religious or political intervention.

Those opposing abortion are mostly firm believers in Christianity, who advocate that the Christian faith should be reflected in politics and education. Some of them are so adamant that they carry out terrorist acts against abortion clinics.

Religious differences are often directly tied with differences between races. Religious confrontation has often inflamed racial prejudice. But cases of blatant discrimination based on religion or race have become much fewer since the establishment of civil rights in 1964.

American Social Problems

Q: How serious is the drug problem in the USA?

According to 2008 statistics, the total number of drug-related arrests reached 1,304,100. If one adds the number of people involved in serious drug-related crimes, the figure soars.

In the bigger cities there are places called "shooting galleries," where people meet secretly and shoot each other up with drugs. Strong drugs like "crack" smuggled from Latin America are freely available there. A single hit costs about $20, but once a person is addicted, he or she can lose everything in the need to buy more, and whole families are destroyed. Also, people share injection needles, which heightens the risk of AIDS infection, another social problem.

For the poorer segments of society, drugs are not only a method of escaping from the pain of daily existence, but also, if one belongs to a gang, a way to earn considerable amounts of cash. The number of people who enter the drug business and get involved

Chapter 5 Society—Life

in gang disputes, eventually getting killed or being sent to prison, is increasing.

Drugs is one the most serious problems gnawing away at American society.

Q: What kinds of social problems does racial confrontation cause in the US?

Racial confrontation can be the cause of tragic incidents and disturbances. Confrontations between whites and blacks or other minority groups have been behind many violent incidents. One example occurred in May of 1992, when riots erupted in Los Angeles minutes after an all-white jury acquitted LA police officers on charges of beating a black man. Sections of the city were burnt to ashes by angry rioters.

But the most serious element is probably the distrust that still exists among races in US society—even when it doesn't develop into riots. There are psychological aspects to the problem which resist statistic analysis, making easy solutions impossible. And since suspicion and distrust do exist, incidents can develop out of the slightest matters.

Injuring others or discriminating against them on racial grounds is strictly prohibited by law. Yet crimes related to racial discrimination never cease, which shows just how deep-rooted racial problems are in the US. For example, 6,604 crimes related to racial, religious, and gender discrimination were reported by the FBI in 2009.

Q: What is the status of gun control in the US?

There were 14,299 murder victims in the US in 2008. Roughly 70% of these were killed by a gun. The opinion that people have the right to possess guns in the US remains strong. The reasons behind it stem from the fact that Americans won independence from Britain with arms, and in the pioneer period guns were necessary for self-protection and hunting.

For all that, an increase of atrocious crimes has led Congress to pass a bill stipulating that gun-sellers must urge buyers to reconsider at the time of purchase. Some areas like New York do enforce strict gun control laws. Others like Texas completely oppose gun control, which shows no chance of advance there.

Gun control is a difficult issue in the US. Public opinion is strung between individual rights and the public welfare.

Q: What is the current state of crime in the US?

The serious crime problem in the US has been reported many times in Japan. Particularly troubling are the crimes involving guns and drugs, race-related and sex-related crimes, and crimes against defenseless members of society, like children. According to 2008 statistics, arrests for crimes totaled 11.1 million.

In addition to educational or racial problems, mental disorders caused by job loss or stress are becoming another cause of crime. The world is becoming more complex and people feel increasingly alienated, which sometimes leads to tragic incidents. Urban crimes are more serious than ever. Washington, D.C. is a place with a particularly high crime rate: 78 murder cases in a population of 100,000, 56 rapes, and 1,230 cases of burglary.

But we should bear in mind that most of the US is safe with people living there quite peacefully. There is now an intensive political debate among people who advocate the incorporation of stronger law and police power to ensure public order, and people who argue that the funding for such a project would be better spent on welfare and education.

Q: How is the US unemployment rate changing?

Recently, the unemployment rate has been sky-high at 9.6% in 2010. This rivals the unemployment rate of 1982, which at 10.8% holds the record for highest unemployment rate in US history. The current unemployment is due to the economic crash of 2008, from which the US is still recovering.

A closer look at the figures, however, shows the unemployment rate of whites in 2008 as 4.4% while that of blacks was 9.2% and 6.3% for Hispanics. The racial unemployment gap is certainly a long-standing issue.

Family and Community

Q: What kind of community activities are there in the US?

There is a thriving tradition of community activities in the US. Parents participate in activities related to their children's education, taking turns managing the children's basketball team or the Little League on the weekends. They also participate in many other volunteer activities. The centers of these community activities are usually schools or churches, which also, if occasion demands, provide the place for exchanges of views on local issues, such as children's education.

Community activity plays an important role as

the core of democracy in US society. It has its origins in the meetings colonists held to discuss and make decisions about issues affecting the community.

Q: What is the status of volunteer activity in the US?

Americans are very active in volunteer work. Children are encouraged to take part in volunteer activities as a part of their education. Senior citizens also take an active role, using their leisure time for the betterment of society.

A community consciousness and the desire to contribute underlies this volunteer work. Activities include taking care of patients and cleaning at local hospitals, participating in children's education at schools, distributing food to the homeless, and helping at welfare facilities.

Companies are also enthusiastic in making their own kind of contribution. They raise funds, and frequently donate part of their revenues for welfare or museum management. Those corporate activities seem to have something in common with the spirit of volunteering.

Q: What are "family values"?

"Family values" have been the subject of much public

debate, and in 1992 they even became a Republican slogan in the presidential election. The restoration of such "family values" was seen as the solution for current social problems. The epitome of "family values" was the traditional American family: a hardworking, pious father and mother with children who respect their parents, attend school, and actively participate in community work. The break-down of the family was seen as the key to the run-down state of education, juvenile crime, and the degeneration of the community.

But the theme of "family values" also became the target of criticism: people said it was out of touch with reality, enforced old values, and ran counter to ideas of gender equality—women should work on equal terms in society, and not just live to be mothers.

Other people criticized the simple-minded advocacy of family values as a vain attempt to turn back the clock and put the lid on the real problems in American society.

What is clear from all these differing opinions is that the great majority of American people felt disorientation in a society that was rapidly changing. They felt they were losing the "family values" the Republicans advocated. Putting aside questions of worth, such discussion surrounding "family values" highlights the most serious problems facing American

Chapter 5 Society—Life

society today: the increase in crime, problems in education, and social alienation.

Q: What is the real status of the breakdown of the family in the US?

The high divorce rate is probably the most egregious indication of the breakdown of the family in America. According to statistics in 2009, 2,077,000 got married, while almost 5 out of every 1,000 people got divorced. This trend has continued since the 1980s—which means, roughly speaking, that half the number of couples who marry later divorce.

As a result, many children are not raised by dual-parent families. Many reasons are conceivable for the high divorce rate. One of them may be women's advancement in society, and an increasing affluence making it less necessary for a family to stick together. There is also a general tendency to give great value to self-assertion, which does not necessarily work in the context of marriage.

Q: Who is "Generation X"?

The term "Generation X" is very much like the Japanese buzzword "shin-jinrui" ("new human being"). Generation X refers to the generation that came after the "angry generation" represented by the anti-war and Hippie movements in the 1960s and 1970s. They are the post-Baby Boomer generation, those who grew up watching TV in the post-Vietnam War era when fears were growing about America's social and economic decline.

Generation Xers typically spend weekends at the shopping mall with friends, or immerse themselves in the computer when alone. They are cool and cynical about things, not having found anything in particular to believe in or devote themselves to. The generation was so named by the novelist Douglas Coupland.

It is not clear whether the term is one of criticism, used by the older generation against the younger, or simply denotes a change in values and society. What is clear is that these so-called Generation Xers are now becoming the core of American society.

People and Nature

Q: What does nature mean to Americans?

In general, ever since they immigrated to the New World, Americans have fought against nature, conquered it, expanded frontiers, cultivated land, and laid railways. How to control nature was their perpetual preoccupation, which developed into a belief in material civilization and the science-is-everything attitude.

Such a stance is in contradiction to various countries in Asia, where people seek instead to merge themselves in nature, and where a particular value of coexistence with nature has arisen.

However, as the environment in America has suffered increasing devastation, and more attention has been given to health problems such as obesity, a shift has occurred in people's attitude toward nature. For years now there have been nationwide—and now worldwide—movements for environmental protection and preservation. These movements have led to the protection of endangered fauna and flora, and a widescale return to organic agriculture and consumption of natural foods.

Q: What are the environmental pollution regulations in the US?

Various laws have been established in the US for environmental protection. To take one example, in some communities and states bonfires in one's yard are prohibited. One must get permission to fish, and there are limitations on the amount of fish and shellfish one can catch and take home.

Nonetheless, serious environmental pollution exists in some places in the US. For example, Los Angeles can become so laden with heavy smog that it sometimes appears to be covered in fog. The California government is forever trying out new laws and legal restrictions in order to remedy this problem. One such regulation set up carpool lanes giving priority to vehicles shared by two or more passengers, in an attempt to decrease the number of vehicles on the freeways. Companies also make pro-environmental products or simplified packages as part of their marketing strategies.

In addition to these joint efforts on the part of the government and the public, general support for environmental protection is very strong in the US, and exerts a large influence in government policymaking.

Chapter 5 Society—Life

The Obama administration even campaigned on the development of green policies and industries during the presidential election of 2008.

Even so, opinion varies as to how far environmental issues should be given priority, especially when policies threaten a convenient and comfortable lifestyle—as seen in California cases where bills with strong restrictions are often shelved.

The US has the largest number of planes and cars in the world, and the nation is a consumer of diverse goods. To face up to the environmental problem squarely means to reconsider the country's entire lifestyle.

Q: Why do Americans feel so much affection for dolphins and whales?

An international treaty to prohibit whaling was established when the number of whales in the world decreased dramatically due to unrestrained hunting. During the whale protection campaign, the whale became a symbol of wildlife protection in general. The same is true of the dolphin. Animated films and TV programs on dolphins that showed their advanced intelligence made the dolphin a popular ocean creature.

In fact, whale hunting was once carried out by the US, particularly in the mid-nineteenth century, when

US whaling ships sailed the world. One of the reasons Perry asked Japan to open the country was to gain access to Japanese ports for American ships to harbor.

Americans used whale oil for making candles, not for food. Once electricity was invented, therefore, the need to catch whales disappeared, and whales became relatively unimportant for them. They thus had no objection to the prohibition of whaling.

Whales and dolphins have gained the status of symbols of animal protection and environmental preservation in the US today. Raising any question about the appropriateness of whaling restrictions is almost a taboo subject.

Chapter 6

Culture & Customs

American Art

Q: What was American art in the nineteenth century like?

Most European immigrants who came to America before the nineteenth century lived a simple life in the New World that had little if any involvement with art. In those days, most paintings were copies of European paintings, and usually landscapes or portraits. But even as most artists copied European styles, they also explored the vast world of nature in the new continent. They tried to capture its grand mountains and forests on canvas. The paintings of this time, which are realistic but also grand and imbued with a glowing light, are reminiscent of religious pictures. One gets an idea of the way in which these Europeans who had come across the ocean and cultivated the land thought of the new continent as "the Promised Land." These landscape painters are referred to as the Hudson River group.

Chapter 6 Culture & Customs

Q: What were the main events in American art in the twentieth century?

In the twentieth century, waves from the various artistic revolutions that took place in European art reached US shores too. People of wealth, like Guggenheim, brought works of art over to America, and in time the ground was prepared for the introduction of contemporary paintings.

Movements to paint American landscapes and still life in various styles arose, actively supported by museums. The Whitney Museum in New York is one example.

By the end of WWI, many artists congregated in New York, including Impressionists, Dadaists, and even Abstract artists. This trend continued into the 1930s and 1940s, and even later. More artists came over from Europe to settle, adding their influences, which led to the further growth of American art.

The most notable thing about this period is that it is when US commercial art first took root and flourished. The designs and architecture of Art Deco with its modern simplicity suited the age of mass production. It captured people's imagination so much that Art Deco was soon seen in many urban settings. Not long after WWII, new paintings started being produced that used aspects of advertisements and commercial products.

Q: What is Pop art?

Pop art dominated a generation. It was one of the largest movements of art in twentieth-century America. The early twentieth century had already seen the development of Dadaism, which debunked conventional ideas and brought "things" ("*objets*") over into the world of art. It had also seen Cubism, which brought bold changes to previous ideas about perspective and color. All sorts of art developed out of these styles, and they flourished in the US too.

Pop art developed from the merging of new means of expression, with industrial art directed toward the masses. Representative artists of Pop art are Andy Warhol, with his paintings of Coke bottles, and Roy Lichtenstein, with his famous printing dot pictures. A certain irony and mocking of society can be detected in their work, as well as a strong and vibrant American energy. Pop art spread all over the world as an art that merged traditional elements with mass culture and absorbed the energy and contradictions of society. It was an art that expressed itself exuberantly and naturally, without clinging to the ways of the past.

American Entertainment and Show Business

Q: How has Disney affected American culture?

It was in 1928 that Walt Disney, a man from Kansas who had come to Hollywood, had his big hit with his character of Mickey Mouse. Thereafter, he introduced a succession of characters like Donald Duck and Snow White, and his cartoons became popular all over America.

Walt Disney produced cartoons which captured children's imaginations. His depiction of sweet, attractive characters reached a wide audience through films and subsequently TV, causing a sensation in the world of American animation.

Disneyland and Disney World in Florida were gigantic enterprises. They reproduced the world of animation in the real world, and they provided a fantasy world in a man-made setting. This was uniquely American.

Q: How did the American movie industry develop?

American movies are almost synonymous with Hollywood. In the beginning, however, movies were mainly produced in New York, and in fact, some movies are still produced there. It was in the 1910s that filmmakers went out one after another to Hollywood. The climate there was more conducive to year-round shooting. Also, at the time it was just a vast farmland inherited by settlers, and it offered the chance of liberation from the various fetters that impeded the business in New York.

The 1920s and 1930s were a golden era for the American film industry. Movies were an important source of entertainment for Americans living scattered all across the vast land. People loved being able to see the splendid stage sets of Broadway in the movies, as well as seeing thrilling Westerns. Many talented people came to America from Europe seeking to produce entertainment in a country where they would be backed by more capital.

The movie industry declined with TV's rise in popularity. But that downtrend has recently been stayed by the large-scale movies produced through computer technology. Nevertheless, Hollywood is often criticized for being too commercially oriented, and for making movies with too many scenes of sex and violence at the expense of subtle, nuanced emotion. In that sense the urbane movies that used to be produced in New York are sorely missed.

Q: What is a Broadway musical?

The Broadway musical typifies New York show business. Many musical theaters are concentrated around the Times Square area where Broadway and Seventh Avenue intersect. Because of this, "Broadway" has become almost synonymous with the word "musical."

Musicals were first introduced around 1860 as shows that combined popular drama and music in a lighter way than opera. It was not until the early twentieth century that musicals really found a stronghold and started being frequently performed. The emergence of that uniquely American music jazz also helped musicals gain a following. Masters of American music like George Gershwin (composer of "Porgy and Bess") and Leonard Bernstein (composer of "West Side Story") also lent their support to musicals and further enriched the form.

The musical is neither simply opera nor ballet, but a composite art form born in America in which both music and dance can be enjoyed on the same stage. Though musicals target a mass audience, the performances are of the highest sophistication.

Competition is intense, and a single negative review in a newspaper can decrease audiences dramatically, sometimes leading to the cancellation of a show's run.

American Music

Q: What is the history of American classical music?

The first professional American composer is said to be Stephen Foster (1826–1864), the composer of "Old Black Joe" and other masterpieces. He incorporated tunes played by early settlers into a style that is uniquely American. Somebody who became interested in this type of American music was Antonin Dvorak, who was invited to New York in the late nineteenth century as a visiting music professor.

In nineteenth-century America, however, classical music was still considered to be music from Europe for the leisured classes. It had no general popularity. Dvorak put great effort into nurturing students, and in fact one of his student's students was George Gershwin. With the booming economy in the 1920s, musicals performed for the public came into vogue, and Jazz, which originated in African American culture, attained a place in the culture.

Gershwin incorporated all that kind of music, as well as all the noises of the city—even cars honking—into his music, which became very successful. American classical music continued to develop its own unique territory, absorbing the energy of popular music. Leonard Bernstein, the conductor and musical director of the New York Philharmonic Orchestra, also made a tremendous contribution.

The famous Carnegie Hall in New York City.

Q: What is country music?

Country music has its origins in the folk music sung by Scottish settlers in the Appalachian Mountains. This folk music developed into the country and western music we know now with the influence of blues and other "black music" from the South.

The banjo (which has its origins in an African folk-music instrument) and the rhythms and lyrics of the blues were all incorporated into country music, which gained great popularity. In the 1930s it became associated with then-fashionable western movies, creating a fixed association of the cowboy with the country song.

Today, country music has a steady following, similar to the enka in Japan. The subjects of country music are usually lovers, mothers, or life in prison. Some songs are very much like modern renditions of stories surrounding the lonely outsider cowboy.

Q: How did Jazz and Blues develop?

Jazz was born in New Orleans as African American music. It seems to have originated with the bands composed of Creoles and mulattos who played on the stage in bars. In 1917, when the US entered WWI and New Orleans became a military harbor, the entertainment section of the city was closed, and strict official discipline was enforced. Musicians lost their jobs and moved up north along the Mississippi to Kansas City and Chicago. Along with them came jazz and blues (the base of jazz), which then spread to other parts of America.

Q: What is the generation of Rock 'n' Roll?

The 1950s were the golden age of affluence in America. A new mass music was born in this period, with its

CHAPTER 6 CULTURE & CUSTOMS

basis in the melody and rhythm of jazz and blues, but influenced too by country music and other popular music, played at a fast tempo by white groups. This music was Rock 'n' Roll. With the appearance of the superstar Elvis Presley, this music took the world by storm in the 1950s and early 1960s.

Elvis Presley is accredited with igniting the Rock 'n' Roll era.

Rock 'n' Roll was later influenced by the anti-war and other social movements, and it underwent further change with the British sensation, The Beatles. It then became "rock music."

Rock 'n' Roll became rock music at a time when American society was undergoing enormous change. The 1950s was the period called Pax Americana, when American values had sway all over the world. But in the 1960s, Pax Americana was questioned in the protests by new generations born after the war. Dissatisfaction about the Vietnam War and anger about racial discrimination toward blacks led to criticism of American values and power. An intense social movement developed in many places.

Rock music reflects the voice of young people at this turning point in American history.

Q: How was "Rap" music created?

Towards the end of the 1980s, a more narrative-type vocalization in music, backed by strong rhythms, became popular among black people. This music, called "Rap," has now become the mainstream black music.

Most rap music has a distinctive rhythm. Rappers express their political stance, social dissatisfaction, and demands, incorporating many slang expressions into their songs. Some rap music has a strongly cynical and even anti-social message. It is like a scream of agony from black society, which has experienced so much disparity in wealth, and suffers from crime and drugs. Some rap bands have members in prison with life sentences.

Besides carrying a strong political message to the world, rap music is also an expression of black fashion and culture. Its popularity among white people has increased tremendously over the years.

Rap, a type of music with strong rhythms and narrative-type lyrics, is a truly American invention.

National Culture and Regional Culture

Q: Are there any cowboys left in America?

Cowboys were originally cattle herders, people who transferred cattle to and from the settlements to the railways in the late nineteenth century, when the wilderness was being developed.

The concept of the "cowboy" arose from early times, when men were hired to herd cattle from farm to farm.

It was the cowboys' job to protect cattle from theft and attack as they drove them to their destination. It was a harsh job. Many cowboys got injured, or involved in fights along the way, or became ill and died. There were many drifters in their number, the type who often appear in Westerns, and these also included some very violent men. The image of cowboys roaming the wilderness, however, became gradually idealized in movies and stories as a symbol of the American pioneer.

"Cowboy" is now an epithet used to refer to any man with a slightly rustic air, but who is honest and gentle, and physically strong—with a hint of loneliness. Today such cowboys are becoming ever more urbane and intellectual.

The decline of the cowboy attests to the changes that have taken place in industry and society in America.

Q: What do Levi's jeans symbolize?

In March 1977, a pair of Levi's jeans dating from the end of the nineteenth century were auctioned off for $25,000. The very popular blue jeans originated from a pair of pants made of tent fabric by Levi Strauss, who came to California to look for a gold mine during the Gold Rush. The $25,000 jeans apparently belonged to somebody doing work that involved riding, at the frontier or the mines.

Jeans are indeed a symbol of the sweat and hard work of people who came across the ocean and crossed the continent, overcoming poverty to build the new country. Now jeans prevail all over the world, an American export. They are an item of clothing that symbolize the casual and carefree culture of Americans and the indomitable spirit of their immigrant ancestors.

CHAPTER 6 CULTURE & CUSTOMS

Q: What kind of American culture does Las Vegas represent?

Las Vegas was first founded by Spanish explorers, as a watering place in the desert.

Today, the city has been transformed by great wealth into a glittering city in the sands. It seems an apt symbol of the traditional American idea that man can master and tame nature.

If one drives across the desert toward Las Vegas at night, the first thing one sees is a glow, which then overwhelms one in a great flood of light as one gets nearer. All kinds of hotels of various tastes stand in an ocean of neon lights. In some places, one can even take photos at night without a flash.

Las Vegas is a town made solely for the pursuit of amusements like gambling and leisure activities. This happened because the state of Nevada officially approved gambling. Nevada is also a state where it is very easy to get married and divorced: there are as many as fifty drive-through (not drive-in) wedding halls. Amazingly, even prostitution is legal in this state. A certain brazen practicality is evident here. This is after all, a city for people looking for wealth and amusement.

Las Vegas became known as a place for gambling because of lax gambling laws in Nevada.

Many casino-hotels even added large-scale attractions for children in order to attract whole families as guests. Many companies, including high-tech firms, have also moved in.

Historically, many Americans wanted to live in Las Vegas. However, after the economic crash of 2008, the population growth in Las Vegas has declined. Although the city's population growth used to be one of the highest in the states at 26% per year, the US Census Bureau has detected a steep decline in the number of people moving there. In 2010, the total population of the city and its suburbs was 1,951,269.

Food Culture

Q: Is Coca-Cola still representative of American food culture?

Coca-Cola is Americans' favorite soft drink. Some people even drink Coca-Cola for breakfast.

Coca-Cola ("Coke") was first made in 1886 by a pharmacist in Atlanta, Georgia, in his own backyard as a tonic. His sales at that time averaged nine bottles a day. He later sold the product rights, and a new investor started to sell the beverage on a large scale in 1899 as a soft drink.

A Coca-Cola truck displays the Coca-Cola logo known all over the world.

Coca-Cola was not simply a delicious beverage, however. Its advertisements and methods of promotion were precursors of the age of mass consumption that exists in America today. Its unique bottle shape, logo, and image of women drinking it for refreshment gained it a hold in the public imagination.

After WWII, Coke spread all over the globe. Many people disapproved of this, and spoke of the phenomenon as "Cocacolanization." Like it or not, however, Coca-Cola was a product that symbolized how much American culture had permeated the world. The Coca-Cola Company has 43% of the domestic market share in soft drinks, according to a 2008 report by Beverage Digest. Coca-Cola Classic, the original brand, has 1/5 of the total soft drink market.

Q: What is the national food of America?

Driving along freeways, one sees countless billboards for McDonald's and Burger King. They are favorite places to eat. French fries are a must with hamburgers. Actually, hamburgers and French fries are the most-ordered fast food in the US.

A hamburger and fries are the most frequently ordered fast foods in America.

Many wealthier people in urban areas turn up their noses at fast-food restaurants. But such people still use hamburgers for barbecues, which many have in summer in their country cottages.

Q: What is a "California Roll"?

A "California roll" is a kind of American sushi, with avocado at the center and rolled seaweed on the inside (usually the seaweed, or nori, is on the outside). Sushi arrived in the US and gained popularity in the early 1980s. The number of Japanese restaurants increased, and now in the cities they are just as popular as Italian or Chinese restaurants.

With the increase of Japanese restaurants came the invention of several types of American-style sushi. The California Roll is one of these, available at most Japanese restaurants in the US.

American Holidays

Q: What kind of events take place on Independence Day?

On Independence Day large firework displays are held in many places in the US. Other holidays are often switched to make the weekend longer, but July 4, the birthday of the nation, is never switched. The only other holidays that are not altered are Christmas and New Year's Days. To Americans, Independence Day is as important a day as these.

Q: What is Martin Luther King, Jr. Day?

This national holiday is a memorial day for Rev. Martin Luther King, Jr., the African American leader and key figure in the Civil Rights movement. It is his birthday, though in fact it falls on the third Monday of every January.

The motion to make this day a memorial day was first made during the civil rights movements. However, some people of other races, particularly conservative whites, were opposed to the idea. Debate continued for some years about whether to observe this memorial day nationally. Today Martin Luther King, Jr. Day is an important holiday, and many government offices and companies close.

Martin Luther King, Jr.

Q: What kind of holidays are Memorial Day and Labor Day?

Memorial Day is the last Monday of May. It is held in memory of the war dead. Labor Day is the first Monday in September and is held to honor workers. It is customary to make the period between Memorial Day and Labor Day the summer holiday season, and many people take their summer vacation during this period.

Q: What are the origins of Halloween?

On October 31st, children dress up as ghosts, monsters, and other costumes and make the rounds of their neighborhoods asking for candy. People make lanterns out of big pumpkins by scooping out the flesh, and carve them into the heads of goblins. This

Chapter 6 Culture & Customs

custom is said to have its origins in the old Celtic belief that the God of Death comes to carry off the souls of the dead. When it was brought to the US it combined with the eve of the Catholic All Saints Day. It is now one of the most fun and exciting celebrations for children.

Children wearing costumes on Halloween.

Q: What kind of holiday is Thanksgiving Day?

Thanksgiving Day originates in the celebratory meal held by the first pilgrims to America, the people who came on the Mayflower. They had a big feast to thank God for their first autumn harvest in Plymouth Colony. It became on official holiday only after the US became independent. In 1941 it began to be celebrated on the fourth Thursday of November.

Thanksgiving Day is a very significant holiday for Americans. Families gather and eat a dinner of roasted turkey and pumpkin pie, just like their forefathers did, and pray for good health.

Thanksgiving Day is also the day that many businesses start their Christmas sales campaigns. The day after Thanksgiving is actually the start of the year-end season.

Q: What does Christmas mean to Americans?

Christmas is the most important holiday in the whole year for most Americans. Not only is it a religious holiday, but it is also a festival that has a big influence on the economy. In the period between Thanksgiving and Christmas Day, Americans do Christmas shopping, and hold parties—the whole of America indulge in consumption. 30% of annual retail sales are said to fall in this season, which is very important for retailers, restaurants, and the travel business.

Q: What are the Jewish holy days?

The Jewish holy days are days designated in the Old Testament as sacred to the Jewish people. Two important ones are Passover, in April, which celebrates the Jewish Exodus from Egypt, and Hanukkah ("Festival of Lights"), in December, which commemorates the rededication of the Temple in Jerusalem. Many urban offices where Jewish people work are closed on such holidays.

American Sports

Q: What are the four major professional sports of America?

Baseball, American football, basketball, and ice hockey are the largest-scale professional sports. They are the Four Major Pro Sports.

Canada also has professional teams in all these sports except for American football. Canadian baseball and hockey teams participate in the American league.

An American baseball stadium.

It is customary to sing the national anthem before games. When a Canadian team participates, both anthems are sung.

Q: How popular is American football?

American football is a very popular sport. It could even be called the national sport. Originating in British Rugby but developing into something quite different, it became a professional sport in 1895.

According to Harper's Index, the TV audience of the 1996 Super Bowl Final exceeded the votes cast in the presidential election of the same year. More than 43 million people watched the fierce contest between the Dallas Cowboys and the Pittsburgh Steelers.

American football is one of the most popular professional sports in America.

Football is a game where each team player has his own role, and players crash violently into each other. Yet even though individual play is encouraged, the whole team has to move and work together. Football can thus be said to share much in common with American business practices. Actually, many Americans have had some experience of football, either as players or as spectators, at school. It is thus not too much to say that this sport has had a formative affect on them.

Q: Where does basketball get its mass of support?

Basketball is particularly popular among African Americans in the US. The fact that this sport does not require a large space nor large amounts of money—all you need is a ball and a basket—makes it popular among low-income people. Go to any urban area in the states and you will see young people using a patch of waste ground to compete with each other shooting the ball into a basket. Many star basketball players started out like this as youngsters.

Basketball is extremely popular both as a professional and college sport.

Basketball was invented in the winter of 1891 at a college in Springfield, Illinois, as an indoor winter sport. It is the epitome of an American-made sport.

Q: Why hasn't soccer become more popular in the US?

Many immigrants in America come from soccer-loving countries, so it wouldn't be true to say that soccer has no following at all. As a matter of fact, in 1967, professional teams were organized and games were played in a league. The Oakland Clippers won the championship. But unfortunately, the pro league was disbanded after a year. Where the 1994 World Series was held in the US, each football ground was filled to capacity. At the Atlanta Olympics too, the American team received much support when it put up such a good fight.

Soccer games are held across the US today. But probably because of the overwhelming popularity of the Four Major Pro Sports, soccer is not a game that the average American knows much about.

Ice hockey is the only sport among the Four Major Pro Sports that was not made in the USA. It was in fact made in Canada. That soccer was neither made nor developed in the US might be the reason it hasn't gained more of a following. While Americans are generally interested in new things, they can also be quite uninterested in unfamiliar things from other countries. This somewhat contradictory attitude might derive from an "island mentality"—this huge land is after all surrounded by the Atlantic and Pacific Oceans.

Word List

- 本文で使われている全ての語を掲載しています（LEVEL 1、2）。ただし、LEVEL 3以上は、中学校レベルの語を含みません。
- 語形が規則変化する語の見出しは原形で示しています。不規則変化語は本文中で使われている形になっています。
- 一般的な意味を紹介していますので、一部の語で本文で実際に使われている品詞や意味と合っていないことがあります。
- 品詞は以下のように示しています。

名 名詞	代 代名詞	形 形容詞	副 副詞	動 動詞	助動 助動詞
前 前置詞	接 接続詞	間 間投詞	冠 冠詞	略 略語	俗 俗語
頭 接頭語	尾 接尾語	号 記号	関 関係代名詞

A

- **abandon** 動 ①捨てる, 放棄する ②（計画などを）中止する, 断念する
- **abbreviation** 名 ①省略, 短縮 ②略語
- **abhor** 動（ひどく）嫌う
- **ability** 名 ①できること,（～する）能力 ②才能
- **abolish** 動 廃止する, 撤廃する
- **abolishment** 名 廃止, 撤廃
- **abortion** 名 妊娠中絶, 堕胎
- **Abraham Lincoln** エイブラハム・リンカーン《米国第16代大統領, 在任1861–65》
- **absolutely** 副 完全に, 確実に
- **absorb** 動 吸収する
- **abstract** 名 抽象芸術［絵画］
- **abuse** 名 虐待, 悪用, 乱用
- **accelerate** 動 加速する
- **accent** 名 訛り
- **accept** 動 ①受け入れる ②同意する, 認める
- **acceptable** 形 ①受諾しうる ②容認できる
- **acceptance** 名 受諾, 容認
- **access** 熟 gain access to に近づく, に接近する
- **accident** 名 ①（不慮の）事故, 災難 ②偶然
- **acclimatize** 動（気候や環境に～を）慣れさせる
- **accord** 動 一致する
- **accordance** 名 一致, 適合 in accordance with ～に従って
- **according** 副《– to ～》～によれば［よると］
- **accordingly** 副 ①それに応じて, 適宜に ②従って,（～と）いうわけだから
- **accountant** 名 税理士, 会計士
- **accurately** 副 正確に, 正しく, きちんと
- **accuse** 動《– of ～》～（の理由）で告訴［非難］する
- **accused** 動 accuse（告訴する）の過去, 過去分詞 名《the –》被告人
- **achieve** 動 成し遂げる, 達成する, 成功を収める
- **achievement** 名 ①達成, 成就 ②業績
- **acknowledge** 動（～として, ～を）認める

Word List

- **acknowledgment** 名 承認, 同意
- **acquit** 動 〜に無罪判決を言い渡す
- **act** 名 行為, 行い 動 ①行動する ②機能する ③演じる
- **active** 形 ①活動的な ②積極的な ③活動[作動]中の
- **actively** 副 活発に, 活動的に
- **activity** 名 活動, 活気
- **actually** 副 実際に, 本当に, 実は
- **adamant** 形 (意志などが)断固とした, 堅固な
- **add** 動 ①加える, 足す ②足し算をする ③言い添える
- **addict** 動 中毒にさせる, ふけらせる
- **addition** 名 ①付加, 追加, 添加 ②足し算 in addition 加えて, さらに
- **adequate** 形 十分な, ふさわしい, 適切な
- **administer** 動 ①管理する, 運営する ②統治する ③施行する
- **administration** 名 管理, 統治, 政権 Bush Administration ブッシュ政権 Clinton administration クリントン政権 Drug Enforcement Administration 麻薬取締局
- **admittedly** 副 確かに, 認めざるをえないところだが
- **adopt** 動 ①採択する, 選ぶ ②承認する ③養子にする
- **advance** 名 進歩, 前進
- **advanced** 動 advance (進む) の過去, 過去分詞 形 上級の, 先に進んだ, 高等の advanced country 先進国
- **advancement** 名 進歩, 前進, 昇進
- **advantageous** 形 都合のよい, 有利な
- **advertisement** 名 広告, 宣伝 classified advertisement (求人・不動産などの) 案内広告
- **advice** 名 忠告, 助言, 意見
- **advocacy** 名 擁護
- **advocate** 動 主張する, 提唱する
- **affair** 名 ①事柄, 事件 ②《-s》業務, 仕事, やるべきこと
- **affect** 動 ①影響する ②(病気などが)おかす 名 感情, 欲望
- **affection** 名 愛情, 感情
- **affirmation** 名 確約, 断言, 肯定, 確認
- **affirmative action** アファーマティブ・アクション《弱者集団の不利な現状を, 歴史的経緯や社会環境を鑑みた上で是正するための改善措置》
- **affluence** 名 豊かさ, 豊富, 富裕
- **affluently** 副 裕福に
- **afford** 動 《can −》〜することができる, 〜する (経済的・時間的な) 余裕がある
- **Afghanistan** 名 アフガニスタン《国》
- **afloat** 形 浮かんで stay afloat (商売などを) なんとか成り立たせる
- **Africa** 名 アフリカ《大陸》
- **African** 形 アフリカ(人)の 名 アフリカ人
- **after all** やはり, 結局
- **after that** その後
- **after-hours** 形 営業時間外の
- **aftermath** 名 (事件などの) 余波, 影響
- **age** 熟 age of 〜の時代 at the age of 〜歳のときに Ice Age 氷河紀[時代]
- **agent** 名 工作員, 諜報員
- **agony** 名 苦悩, 激しい苦痛
- **agricultural** 形 農業の, 農事の
- **agriculture** 名 農業, 農耕
- **aid** 名 援助, 助け
- **aircraft** 名 飛行機, 航空機
- **airplane** 名 飛行機

AMERICA FAQ

- **Alabama** 名 アラバマ州
- **Alamo** 名 アラモ砦, アラモの戦い (Battle of the Alamo)《テキサス独立戦争中の1836年2月23日3月6日の13日間にメキシコ共和国軍とテキサス分離独立派の間で行われた戦闘》
- **Alaska** 名 アラスカ州
- **Aldrich H. Ames** オルドリッチ・エイムズ《CIA工作員, ソ連KGBの協力者であることが発覚し, 1994年に逮捕された, 1941-》
- **Aleutian Islands** アリューシャン列島
- **Alexander Graham Bell** アレクサンダー・グラハム・ベル《電話技術を開発, 1947-1922》
- **Alexander Hamilton** アレクサンダー・ハミルトン《アメリカ合衆国建国の父の1人。アメリカ合衆国憲法の実際の起草者でアメリカ合衆国憲法コメンタリーの古典『ザ・フェデラリスト』の主執筆者, 1755-1804》
- **alien** 名 外国人 **illegal alien** 不法入国者
- **alienate** 動 (人)を仲間外れにする, 無視する, 避ける
- **alienation** 名 疎外感, 疎遠
- **all** 熟 **after all** やはり, 結局 **all over** ~中で, 全体に亘って, ~の至る所で, 全て終わって, もうだめで **all over the world** 世界中に **all the time** ずっと, いつも, その間ずっと **all the way** ずっと, はるばる, いろいろと **at all events** ともかく, いずれにしても **first of all** まず第一に **go all the way** ずっと, 完全に, 行くところまで行く
- **all-out attack** 総攻撃, 全面攻撃
- **all-white** 形 すべて白人の
- **alley** 名 路地, 裏通り, 小道 **Tornado Alley** 竜巻街道, 竜巻多発地帯
- **alliance** 名 同盟 [国], 協調
- **allocate** 動 割り当てる
- **allow** 動 ①許す,《 – … to ~》…が~するのを可能にする, …に~させておく ②与える
- **ally** 名 同盟国, 味方
- **almanac** 名 暦, 年鑑 **Computer Industry Almanac** コンピュータ・インダストリー・アルマナック《米調査会社》
- **along the way** 途中で, これまでに, この先
- **along with** ~と一緒に
- **alter** 動 (部分的に)変える, 変わる
- **although** 接 ~だけれども, ~にもかかわらず, たとえ~でも
- **altogether** 副 まったく, 全然, 全部で
- **amazingly** 副 驚くべきことに
- **Amazon** 名 アマゾン川, アマゾン・ドットコム
- **amendment** 名 ①改正, 修正 ②(憲法の)改正案
- **America** 名 アメリカ《国名・大陸》
- **American** 形 アメリカ(人)の 名 アメリカ人
- **American league** アメリカンリーグ, ア・リーグ
- **American Revolution** アメリカ革命《18世紀後半にイギリス領だった東部13州が結束し, アメリカ独立戦争を経て, 合衆国を形成するまでを指す》
- **American-made** 形 アメリカ製の
- **American-style** 形 アメリカ式の
- **Americana** 名 **Pax Americana** パックス・アメリカーナ《米国の力による平和》
- **Americanized** 形 アメリカ化されている, アメリカ流になっている
- **amicable** 形 (互いに)友好的な
- **amount** 名 ①量, 額 ②《the – 》合計 動 (総計~に)なる

158

Word List

- **amusement** 名 娯楽, 楽しみ
- **amusing** 形 楽しくさせる, 楽しい
- **Anacreon** 形 **To Anacreon in Heaven**「天国のアナクレオンへ」《アメリカ合衆国国歌「星条旗」になった曲。イギリスの作曲家, ジョン・スタフォード・スミス作》
- **analysis** 名 分析, 解析(学)
- **ancestor** 名 ①祖先, 先祖 ②先人
- **ancient** 形 昔の, 古代の
- **and so** そこで, それだから, それで
- **and so forth** など, その他
- **Andy Warhol** アンディ・ウォーホル《アメリカの画家・版画家・芸術家でポップアートの旗手。1928–1987》
- **anger** 名 怒り
- **Anglo-Saxon** 名 アングロ・サクソン人《英語を母国語とする白人の総称》 **White Anglo-Saxon Protestant** ワスプ《アングルサクソン系白人プロテスタントおよびそれによって構成される階層》
- **animated** 形 アニメの
- **animation** 名 アニメーション, 動画
- **announce** 動 (人に)知らせる, 公表する
- **announcement** 名 発表, アナウンス, 告示, 声明
- **annual** 形 年1回の, 例年の, 年次の
- **another** 熟 **one another** お互い **one after another** 次々に, 1つ[人]ずつ
- **antagonistic** 形 対立する, 敵対する
- **anthem** 名 賛美歌, 賛歌 **national anthem** 国歌
- **Anthony Rossi** アンソニー・ロッシ《トロピカーナの創設者, 1900–1993》

- **anti-social** 形 反社会的
- **anti-terrorist measures** 対テロリスト対策
- **anti-war movement** 反戦運動
- **antiabortionist** 名 (人工)中絶反対(論)者
- **Antonin Dvorak** アントニン・ドヴォルザーク《チェコの作曲家, 1841–1904》
- **anybody** 代 ①《疑問文・条件節で》誰か ②《否定文で》誰も(〜ない) ③《肯定文で》誰でも
- **apart** 副 ①ばらばらに, 離れて ②別にして, それだけで **apart from 〜** を除いては
- **apology** 名 謝罪, 釈明
- **Appalachia** 名 アパラチア地方
- **Appalachian Montains** アパラチア山脈《カナダ南部のニューファンドランド島からアメリカ東部のアラバマ州まで南西に延びる山脈》
- **apparatus** 名 装置, 器具
- **apparently** 副 見たところ〜らしい, 明らかに
- **appeal** 動 訴える 名 魅力, 人気
- **appear** 動 ①現れる, 見えてくる ②(〜のように)見える, 〜らしい **appear to** するように見える
- **appearance** 名 ①現れること, 出現 ②外見, 印象
- **Apple** 名 アップル社
- **application** 名 ①アプリケーション ②適用, 応用
- **apply** 動 あてはまる, 適用する
- **appraisal** 名 評価, 査定
- **appropriateness** 名 妥当性, 適切性
- **approve** 動 賛成する, 承認する
- **approximately** 副 おおよそ, だいたい
- **apt** 形 適切な, ふさわしい
- **architecture** 名 ①建築物(様式)

159

America FAQ

②構成, 構造
- **arena** 名 活動の場
- **argue** 動 ①論じる, 議論する ②主張する
- **argument** 名 議論, 討論
- **arise** 動 ①起こる, 生じる ②起きる, 行動を開始する
- **arisen** 動 arise (起こる) の過去分詞
- **Arizona** 名 アリゾナ州
- **arose** 動 arise (起こる) の過去
- **arrange** 動 ①並べる, 整える ②取り決める ③準備する, 手はずを整える
- **arrest** 名 逮捕
- **arrival** 名 ①到着 ②到達
- **art** 熟 composite art form 総合芸術様式 works of art 芸術作品
- **Art Deco** アール・デコ《ヨーロッパおよびアメリカ (ニューヨーク) を中心に1910年代半ばから1930年代にかけて流行, 発展した装飾の一傾向》
- **artery** 名 動脈, 幹線道路
- **article** 名 ① (法令・誓約などの) 箇条, 項目 ② (新聞・雑誌などの) 記事, 論文
- **artist** 名 芸術家
- **artistic** 形 芸術的な, 芸術 (家) の
- **as** 熟 as a matter of fact 実際は, 実のところ as a result その結果 (として) as a result of ～の結果 (として) as far as ～と同じくらい遠く, ～まで, ～する限り (では) as if あたかも～のように, まるで～みたいに as long as ～する以上は, ～である限りは as many as ～もの数の as much as ～と同じだけ as regards ～に関しては, ～については as such ～など as to ～に関しては, ～については, ～に応じて as well なお, その上, 同様に as well as ～と同様に see ～ as … ～を…と考える such ～ as … …のような～ such as たとえば～, ～のような times as … as A Aの～倍の…
- **ash** 名 灰 burnt to ashes 焼けて灰になる, 全焼する
- **Asia** 名 アジア
- **Asian** 名 アジア人 形 アジアの
- **aside** 副 わきへ (に), 離れて put aside わきに置く
- **aspect** 名 ①状況, 局面, 側面 ②外観, 様子
- **Aspen** 名 アスペン《地名》
- **assassinate** 動 暗殺する
- **assassination** 名 暗殺
- **assert** 動 強く主張する, 断言する
- **assertion** 名 言明, 主張
- **assistance** 名 援助, 支援
- **associate** 動 連合 [共同] する, 提携する 名 仲間, 組合員
- **associated** 形 結び付いた, 関連した
- **association** 名 連想
- **Atlanta** 名 アトランタ《都市名》
- **Atlanta Olympics** アトランタ・オリンピック《アトランタで行われた第26回夏季オリンピック, 1996》
- **Atlantic** 形 大西洋の 名《the –》大西洋
- **Atlantic Charter** 大西洋憲章《1941年8月9日12日に行われた大西洋会談において, イギリス首相のウィンストン・チャーチルと, アメリカ合衆国大統領のフランクリン・ルーズベルトによって調印された憲章》
- **Atlantic Ocean** 大西洋
- **atrocious crime** 凶悪犯罪
- **attack** 動 襲う, 攻める 名 攻撃, 非難
- **attain** 動 達成する, 成し遂げる, 達する
- **attempt** 動 試みる, 企てる 名 試み, 企て, 努力
- **attend** 動 出席する, (学校などに)

通う
- **attention** 名注意, 集中
- **attest** 動証言する, 証明する
- **attitude** 名姿勢, 態度, 心構え
- **attract** 動①引きつける, 引く ②魅力がある, 魅了する
- **attraction** 名引きつけるもの, 出し物, アトラクション
- **attractive** 形魅力的な, あいきょうのある
- **auction off ~ for ...** ~を競売にかけて…ドルで売る
- **audience** 名聴衆, 視聴者
- **authority** 名①権威, 権力, 権限 ②《the -ties》(関係) 当局
- **auto** 車の
- **automaker** 名自動車メーカー
- **automobile** 名自動車
- **automotive** 形自動車の
- **autonomy** 名自治(権), 自治体
- **available** 形利用[使用・入手]できる, 得られる
- **Avenue** 名~通り, ~街
- **average** 名平均(値), 並み 形平均の, 普通の 動平均して~になる
- **aviation** 名航空(機製造)
- **avocado** 名アボカド
- **avoid** 動避ける, (~を)しないようにする
- **aware** 形①気がついて, 知って ②(~の) 認識のある be aware of ~に気がついている
- **awareness** 名認識, 自覚, 意識性, 気づいていること
- **awkward** 形①不器用な, 不格好な ②やっかいな, やりにくい
- **awoke** 動 awake (目覚めさせる)の過去
- **axis** 名軸, 中心線

B

- **Baby Boomer** ベビーブーマー, ベビーブーム世代(の人)《1945年から60年代に生まれた人》
- **back** 熟 clothes on one's back 着の身着のままで
- **backbone** 名背骨
- **background** 名背景, 前歴, 生い立ち
- **backlash** 名反発, 反感
- **backyard** 名裏庭
- **badly** 副①悪く, まずく, へたに ②とても, ひどく
- **bail** 名保釈, 保釈金
- **balance** 名均衡, 平均 checks and balances 抑制と均衡 動釣り合いをとる
- **ballet** 名バレエ, バレエ団
- **ban** 名禁止, 禁制
- **band** 名バンド, 楽団
- **Bangladesh** 名バングラデシュ《国名》
- **banjo** 名バンジョー
- **bank** 名 Federal Reserve Bank 連邦準備銀行 New York Federal Reserve Bank ニューヨーク連邦準備銀行 wildcat bank 山猫銀行《元は人里離れた銀行の意だったが, でたらめが営業を行うものが多かったため不良銀行の代名詞となった》
- **bank note** 紙幣
- **Bank of Japan** 日本銀行, 日銀
- **bankrupt** 形破産した go bankrupt 破産する
- **bankruptcy** 名破産, 倒産
- **banner** 名旗, 垂れ幕 Star-Spangled Banner 星条旗
- **bar** 名酒場
- **Barack Obama** バラク・オバマ《アメリカ合衆国の政治家。第44代大統領, 在任1961-》

America FAQ

- **barbecue** 名 バーベキュー
- **bargaining** 名 交渉, 取引
- **base** 名 基礎, 土台, 本部 **Guantanamo military base** グァンタナモ米軍基地《キューバ東南部のグァンタナモ湾に位置するアメリカ海軍の基地》
- **baseball** 名 ①野球 ②野球用のボール
- **based** 形 ～に拠点のある, ～をベース[基礎]にした **be based on ～** に基づく
- **basically** 副 基本的には, 大筋では
- **basis** 名 ①土台, 基礎 ②基準, 原理 ③根拠 ④主成分
- **basketball** 名 バスケットボール
- **battle** 名 戦闘, 戦い
- **bear** 動 生む, 実をつける **bear arms** 武装する, 戦う **bear in mind that** 心に留める
- **beat** 動 打つ
- **Beatles** 名 ビートルズ《バンド名, リバプール出身のロックグループ, 1950-1970》
- **beginning** 名 初め, 始まり
- **behavior** 名 振る舞い, 態度, 行動
- **behind** 前 ①～の後ろに, ～の背後に ②～に遅れて, ～に劣って 副 ①後ろに, 背後に ②遅れて, 劣って **leave behind** あとにする, ～を置き去りにする
- **being** 動 be (～である)の現在分詞 名 存在, 生命, 人間
- **belief** 名 信じること, 信念, 信用
- **believer** 名 信じる人, 信奉者, 信者
- **belong** 動《 – to ～》～に属する, ～のものである
- **belonging** 動 belong (属する)の現在分詞 名《-s》持ち物, 所有物, 財産
- **benefit** 名 利益, 恩恵

- **Bering Sea** ベーリング海《太平洋の最北部の海域》
- **beset** 動 (しつこく～を)悩ませる
- **besides** 前 ①～に加えて, ～のほかに ②《否定文・疑問文で》～を除いて 副 その上, さらに
- **betterment** 名 改良, 向上
- **beverage** 名 飲み物
- **Beverage Digest** ビバレッジ・ダイジェスト《飲料業界誌》
- **beyond** 前 ～を越えて, ～の向こうに
- **biased** 形 偏見のある, 偏った, 先入観にとらわれた
- **Bible** 名 ①《the -》聖書 ②《b-》権威ある書物, バイブル
- **Bible Belt** バイブル・ベルト《聖書地帯, アメリカ合衆国の中西部から南東部でプロテスタント, キリスト教根本主義, 南部バプテスト連盟, 福音派などが熱心に信仰され地域文化の一部となっている地域》
- **bill** 名 法案
- **Bill Clinton** ビル・クリントン《アメリカ合衆国の政治家, 第42代大統領, 在任1993-2001》
- **billboard** 名 広告板, ビルボード
- **billion** 形 10億の, ばく大な, 無数の 名 10億
- **Bin Laden** (オサマ・)ビン・ラディン《サウジアラビア出身のイスラム過激派テロリスト。アルカイダの司令官, 1957-2011》
- **binding** 形 拘束力のある
- **biologically** 副 生物学的に
- **biology** 名 生物学
- **bit** 名 ①小片, 少量 ②《a –》少し, ちょっと
- **blanket** 名 毛布
- **blatant** 形 あからさまな
- **blessing** 名 恩恵
- **bloc** 名 (国家間の)圏, ブロック

Word List

- **blow** 名 打撃
- **blues** 名 ブルース《音楽》
- **board** 動 乗り込む
- **Boeing** 名 ボーイング《米国の航空機メーカー》
- **bold** 形 勇敢な, 大胆な, 奔放な
- **bombing** 名 爆撃, 爆破
- **bonfire** 名 (祝祭日などの) 大かがり火, たき火
- **boom** 名 ブーム, 急成長
- **Boomer** 名 Baby Boomer ベビーブーマー, ベビーブーム世代 (の人) 《1945年から60年代に生まれた人》
- **booming** 形 好景気の, 成長著しい
- **border** 名 境界, へり, 国境
- **bosom** 熟 in the bosom of ～に抱かれて, ～の内部に
- **boss** 名 上司, 親方, 監督
- **Boston** 名 ボストン《都市名》
- **bound** 熟 bound up with ～と密接な関係のある
- **boundary** 名 境界線, 限界
- **brand** 名 ブランド, 商標, 品種
- **brazen** 形 厚かましい, ずうずうしい
- **break out** 発生する, 急に起こる, (戦争が) 勃発する
- **break-down** 名 断絶, 崩壊
- **breakdown** 名 故障, 衰弱, 挫折
- **bridge** 名 Golden Gate Bridge ゴールデン・ゲート・ブリッジ
- **brilliant** 形 光り輝く, 見事な, すばらしい
- **bring about** 引き起こす
- **Britain** 名 大ブリテン (島)
- **British** 形 ①英国人の ②イギリス英語の 名 英国人
- **British Parliament** イギリス議会
- **Broadway** 名 ブロードウェイ《アメリカの劇場産業の代名詞》
- **bronze** 名 ブロンズ, 青銅
- **bubble** 名 泡, バブル (景気)
- **buck** 名 ドル
- **Buddhism** 名 仏教
- **budget** 名 ①経費 ②予算
- **Buffalo** 名 バッファロー《地名》
- **building** 名 建物, 造物, ビルディング
- **bumpy** 形 でこぼこの多い
- **bureau** 名 ①案内所, 事務所 ②局, 部 **Federal Bureau of Investigation** 連邦捜査局《略称FBI, 米国内の複数の州にまたがる犯罪の捜査, 公安情報の収集を任務とする司法省の捜査部門》 **US Census Bureau** 米国勢調査局
- **Burger King** バーガーキング
- **burglary** 名 住居侵入窃盗
- **burnt** 形 焼いた, 焦げた, やけどした **burnt to ashes** 焼けて灰になる, 全焼する
- **bursting** 名 破裂
- **Bush** 名 ジョージ・W・ブッシュ《アメリカ合衆国の政治家。第43代アメリカ合衆国大統領, 任期2001-2009》
- **Bush Administration** ブッシュ政権
- **business** 熟 on business 仕事で
- **bustle** 名 せわしげな動き
- **but** 熟 not ～ but … …ではなくて… not only ～ but (also) … …だけでなく…もまた
- **buyer** 名 買い手, バイヤー
- **buzzword** 名 業界用語

C

- **cab** 名 タクシー
- **Cabinet** 名 内閣, 閣僚

AMERICA FAQ

- □ **cacti** 名 サボテン (cactusの複数形)
- □ **Cajun cooking** ケージャン料理
- □ **California** 名 カリフォルニア《米国の州》
- □ **California Roll** カリフォルニア・ロール
- □ **California Supreme Court** カリフォルニア最高裁判所
- □ **Californian** 形 カリフォルニアの
- □ **camp** 名 収容所 relocation camp 強制収容所
- □ **campaign** 名 ①キャンペーン (活動, 運動) ②政治運動, 選挙運動 動 運動を起こす
- □ **campaigner** 名 (選挙などの) 運動家, 活動家
- □ **Canada** 名 カナダ《国名》
- □ **Canadian** 形 カナダ (人) の 名 カナダ人
- □ **canal** 名 運河
- □ **cancellation** 名 キャンセル, 取り消し
- □ **cancer** 名 癌
- □ **candidate** 名 立候補者
- □ **candle** 名 ろうそく
- □ **cannot** can (〜できる) の否定形 (=can not)
- □ **canvas** 名 キャンバス
- □ **capability** 名 ①能力, 才能 ②機能, 性能 ③可能性, 将来性
- □ **capable** 形 ①《be - of 〜 [〜ing]》〜の能力 [資質] がある ②有能な
- □ **capacity** 名 ①定員, 容量 ②能力, (潜在的な) 可能性
- □ **capital** 名 ①首都 ②資本 (金) 形 ①資本の ②首都の ③最も重要な
- □ **capital punishment** 極刑, 死刑
- □ **capitalism** 名 資本主義
- □ **capture** 動 捕える
- □ **carbon footprint** 二酸化炭素排出量
- □ **care** 熟 health care 健康保険制度 take care of 〜の世話をする, 〜面倒を見る, 〜を管理する
- □ **career** 名 ①(生涯の・専門的な) 職業 ②経歴, キャリア
- □ **carefree** 形 のんきな, 心配のない
- □ **Caribbean** 形 カリブ人, カリブ海
- □ **Caribbean Sea** カリブ海
- □ **carpool** 名 自動車 [マイカー] の相乗り
- □ **carry off** 誘いかける, さらって行く, 運び去る
- □ **carry out** 外へ運び出す, [計画を] 実行する
- □ **Carter** 名 (ジミー・) カーター《第39代アメリカ合衆国大統領, 在任 1977-1981》
- □ **cartoon** 名 時事風刺漫画, アニメ映画
- □ **carve** 動 彫る, 彫刻する
- □ **Cascade Range** カスケード山脈
- □ **cash** 名 現金
- □ **casino-hotel** 名 カジノ付きホテル
- □ **Caspian Sea** カスピ海
- □ **cast** 動 投げる cast a shadow (暗い) 影を落とす 名 votes cast 投票総数
- □ **casual** 形 略式の, カジュアルな
- □ **casualty** 名 死傷者, 犠牲者
- □ **catch sight of** 熟 〜を見つける, 〜を見かける
- □ **Catholic** 形 カトリックの 名 カトリック教徒
- □ **Catholic All Saints Day** 諸聖人の日《カトリック教会の祝日》
- □ **Catholicism** 名 カトリック教義 [信仰]
- □ **cattle** 名 畜牛, 家畜

164

WORD LIST

- □ **caught** 熟 get caught 逮捕される
- □ **cautious** 形 用心深い, 慎重な
- □ **cease** 動 やむ, やめる, 中止する
- □ **ceasefire** 名 休戦, 停戦
- □ **cedar** 名 ヒマラヤスギ, レバノン杉
- □ **ceiling** 名 ①天井 ②上限, 最高価格
- □ **celebrate** 動 ①祝う, 祝福する ②祝典を開く
- □ **celebration** 名 ①祝賀 ②祝典, 儀式
- □ **celebratory** 形 祝賀の
- □ **Celtic** 形 ケルトの
- □ **census** 名 一斉調査, 国勢調査 US Census Bureau 米国勢調査局
- □ **cent** 名 ①セント《米国などの通貨単位。1ドルの100分の1》②《単位としての》100
- □ **central** 形 中央の, 主要な
- □ **Central American** 中米の
- □ **ceremony** 名 ①儀式, 式典 ②礼儀, 作法, 形式ばること
- □ **certain** 形 ①確実な, 必ず~する ②(人が)確信した ③ある ④いくらかの
- □ **certainly** 副 ①確かに, 必ず ②《返答に用いて》もちろん, そのとおり, 承知しました
- □ **chairman** 名 委員長, 会長, 議長
- □ **chairperson** 名 委員長, 会長, 議長
- □ **challenge** 名 ①挑戦 ②難関 動 挑む, 試す
- □ **championship** 名 選手権(試合)
- □ **Chang Jiang** 長江, 揚子江
- □ **change with** 熟 ~とともに変化する
- □ **chaotic** 形 大混乱の, 雑然とした, 混沌とした
- □ **chapter** 名 (書物の)章
- □ **character** 名 (小説・劇などの)登場人物
- □ **characteristic** 名 特徴, 特性, 特色, 持ち味
- □ **characterize** 動 (~を…と)述べる, 特徴づける
- □ **charge** 名 非難, 告発 on charges of ~の罪で
- □ **Charleston** 名 チャールストン《都市名》
- □ **Charter** 名 憲章 Atlantic Charter 大西洋憲章《1941年8月9日12日に行われた大西洋会談において, イギリス首相のウィンストン・チャーチルと, アメリカ合衆国大統領のフランクリン・ルーズベルトによって調印された憲章》UN Charter 国連憲章
- □ **chat** 名 video chat ビデオチャット
- □ **checks and balances** 抑制と均衡
- □ **chemical** 形 化学の, 化学的な 名 化学製品[薬品]
- □ **Chicago** 名 シカゴ《都市名》
- □ **chief** 名 頭, 長, 親分
- □ **China** 名 中国
- □ **Chinatown** 名 中華街
- □ **Chinese** 形 中国(人)の 名 ①中国人 ②中国語
- □ **Chippewa** 名 チペワ族《北米先住民》
- □ **Christian** 名 キリスト教徒, クリスチャン 形 キリスト(教)の
- □ **Christianity** 名 キリスト教, キリスト教信仰
- □ **Christmas** 名 クリスマス
- □ **Christmas Day** クリスマス
- □ **Christopher Columbus** クリストファー・コロンブス《イタリアの航海家, 1492年バハマ諸島を発見, 1451-1506》
- □ **chronic** 形 (病気が)慢性の
- □ **Chrysler** 名 クライスラー《社名》
- □ **Church of Jesus Christ of**

America FAQ

- **Latter-day Saints** 末日聖徒イエスキリスト教会《俗称はモルモン教》
- ☐ **CIA** 略 中央情報局《海外での情報収集, 政治工作を担当する米大統領直属機関》
- ☐ **Cincinnati** 名 シンシナティ《地名》
- ☐ **circle** 名 円, 円周, 輪
- ☐ **circumstance** 名 ①(周囲の)事情, 状況, 環境 ②《-s》(人の)境遇, 生活状態 **extenuating circumstances** 酌量すべき事情[状況]
- ☐ **cite** 動 言及する, 引用する
- ☐ **citizen** 名 ①市民, 国民 ②住民, 民間人
- ☐ **citizenship** 名 公民権, 市民権
- ☐ **civil** 形 ①一般人の, 民間(人)の ②国内の, 国家の ③礼儀正しい
- ☐ **civil lawsuit** 民事訴訟
- ☐ **civil rights movement** 公民権運動
- ☐ **civil war** 内戦, 内乱
- ☐ **Civil War** 南北戦争《1861–1865》
- ☐ **civilian** 形 民間の, 文民の
- ☐ **civilization** 名 文明, 文明人(化)
- ☐ **claim** 動 ①主張する ②要求する, 請求する
- ☐ **clash** 名 (意見, 利害の)衝突
- ☐ **classic** 名 古典
- ☐ **classical** 形 古典の, クラシックの
- ☐ **classified advertisement** (求人・不動産などの)案内広告
- ☐ **clear** 形 ①はっきりした, 明白な ②澄んだ ③(よく)晴れた
- ☐ **cliche** 名 決まり文句, 定型表現
- ☐ **climate** 名 気候, 風土, 環境
- ☐ **cling** 動 くっつく, しがみつく, 執着する
- ☐ **clinic** 名 診療所
- ☐ **Clinton** 名 (ビル・)クリントン《アメリカ合衆国第42代大統領, 在任1993–2001》
- ☐ **Clinton administration** クリントン政権
- ☐ **close to** 《be –》〜に近い
- ☐ **closure** 名 閉鎖, 締め切り, 閉店, 閉会
- ☐ **clothes on one's back** 着の身着のままで
- ☐ **clothing** 名 衣類, 衣料品
- ☐ **cluster** 名 (密集した動物の)群れ, 一団
- ☐ **co-exist** 動 共存する
- ☐ **coast** 名 海岸, 沿岸
- ☐ **coastal** 形 沿岸の, 海岸線に沿った
- ☐ **coastline** 名 海岸線
- ☐ **Coca-Cola** 名 コカコーラ
- ☐ **Coca-Cola Classic** コカコーラ・クラシック
- ☐ **Cocacolanization** 名 コカ・コーラニゼーション《グローバル化現象や文化帝国主義を主に否定的に指す》
- ☐ **coexistence** 名 共存, 共生
- ☐ **Coke** 名 Coca-Colaの別称
- ☐ **Cold War** 冷戦
- ☐ **collaborate** 動 協力する, 共同する, 協調して取り組む
- ☐ **collapse** 名 崩壊, 倒壊
- ☐ **colleague** 名 同僚, 仲間, 同業者
- ☐ **collectively** 副 集合的に
- ☐ **colonial** 形 植民地の
- ☐ **colonist** 名 開拓者, 入植者
- ☐ **colonize** 動 植民する, 入植する
- ☐ **colony** 名 植民[移民](地)
- ☐ **Colorado** 名 コロラド州
- ☐ **colorful** 形 ①カラフルな, 派手な ②生き生きとした
- ☐ **Columbus** 名 (クリストファー・)コロンブス《イタリアの航海家, 1492年バハマ諸島を発見, 1451–1506》

WORD LIST

- **combine** 動 ①結合する[させる] ②連合する, 協力する
- **come** 熟 come about 起こる come across ～に出くわす, ～に遭遇する come after ～のあとを追う come by やって来る, 立ち寄る come into question 問題になる, 議論される
- **comeback** 名 回復, 返り咲き, カムバック
- **comfortable** 形 快適な, 心地いい
- **command** 動 命令する, 指揮する
- **commander** 名 司令官, 指揮官
- **Commander-in-Chief** 名 最高司令官
- **commemorate** 動 ①祝う, 記念する ②賛美する
- **comment** 名 論評, 解説, コメント
- **commerce** 名 商業, 貿易 Department of Commerce 米商務省
- **commercial** 形 商業の, 営利的な
- **commercially** 副 商業的に
- **commit** 動 (罪などを)犯す
- **commitment** 名 委託, 約束, 確約, 責任
- **Commodore Perry** ペリー提督《アメリカ海軍の軍人, 日本の江戸時代に艦隊を率いて鎖国をしていた日本へ来航し, 開国させたことで知られる, 1794~1858》
- **common** 熟 in common (with ～) (～と)共通して
- **communication** 名 伝えること, 伝導, 連絡
- **communist** 名 共産主義者, 共産党員
- **community** 名 ①団体, 共同社会, 地域社会 ②《the -》社会(一般), 世間 ③共有, 共同責任
- **commuter** 形 通勤(通学)の

- **compensation** 名 補償[賠償]金, 埋め合わせ, 補償
- **compete** 動 ①競争する ②(競技に)参加する ③匹敵する
- **competing** 形 競合する
- **competition** 名 競争, 競合, コンペ
- **competitor** 名 競争相手, 競争者
- **complaint** 名 不平, 不満(の種)
- **complete** 動 完成させる
- **completely** 副 完全に, すっかり
- **complex** 形 入り組んだ, 複雑な, 複合の
- **complicated** 形 ①複雑な ②むずかしい, 困難な
- **compose** 動 ①構成する ②作曲する
- **composed** 動 compose (構成する)の過去, 過去分詞
- **composer** 名 作曲家, 作者
- **composite** 形 各種の要素からなる, 合成の, 複合の composite art form 総合芸術様式
- **compound** 名 屋敷
- **comprise** 動 ①(～より)成る ②包含する
- **Computer Industry Almanac** コンピュータ・インダストリー・アルマナック《米調査会社》
- **computer-networked** 形 コンピュータ・ネットワークで結ばれた
- **conceivable** 形 想像できる, 考えられる
- **concentrate** 動 一点に集める[集まる], 集中させる[する]
- **concentration** 名 集中, 集中力, 集合
- **concern** 動 ①関係する,《be -ed in [with] ～》～に関係している ②心配させる,《be -ed about [for] ～》～を心配する 名 ①関心事 ②関心, 心配 ③関係, 重要性

AMERICA FAQ

- **concerned** 形 ①関係している, 当事者の ②心配そうな, 気にしている
- **concerning** 動 concern (関係する) の現在分詞 前 ～についての, 関しての
- **conclude** 動 ①終える, 完結する ②結論を下す
- **condition** 名 ①(健康)状態, 境遇 ②《-s》状況, 様子 ③条件
- **conducive** 動 助けとなる
- **conduct** 動 ①指導する ②実施する, 処理[処置]する
- **conductor** 名 指導者, 案内者, 管理者, 指揮者, 車掌
- **Confederate Army** 南軍
- **Confederation** 同盟, 連合
- **conference** 名 ①会議, 協議, 相談 ②協議会 UN Conference 国連会議
- **confess** 動 (隠し事などを)告白する, 打ち明ける, 白状する
- **confined** 形 閉じ込められた
- **conflict** 名 ①不一致, 衝突 ②争い, 対立 ③論争
- **confront** 動 ①直面する, 立ち向かう ②突き合わせる, 比較する
- **confrontation** 名 対立, 直面
- **conglomeration** 名 集塊, (物の)寄せ集め
- **congregate** 動 集まる, 集合する
- **Congress** 名 アメリカ連邦議会
- **Congressional Republican** 共和党議員
- **connect** 動 つながる, つなぐ, 関係づける
- **Connecticut** 名 コネティカット州
- **connection** 名 ①つながり, 関係 ②縁故
- **conquer** 動 征服する, 制圧する
- **consciousness** 名 意識, 自覚, 気づいていること
- **consent** 名 同意, 承諾, 許可
- **consequence** 名 結果, 成り行き
- **consequently** 副 したがって, 結果として
- **conservative** 形 ①保守的な ②控えめな, 地味な
- **consider** 動 ①考慮する, ～しようと思う ②(～と)みなす ③気にかける, 思いやる
- **considerable** 形 相当な, かなりの, 重要な
- **considerably** 副 かなり, 相当に
- **consideration** 名 ①考慮, 考察 ②考慮すべきこと
- **consist** 動 ①《- of ～》(部分・要素から)成る ②《- in ～》～に存在する, ～にある
- **constitute** 動 構成する, 成す
- **constitution** 名 ①憲法, 規約 ②構成, 構造
- **construct** 動 建設する, 組み立てる
- **construction** 名 構造, 建設, 工事, 建物
- **consumer** 名 消費者
- **consumption** 名 ①消費, 消費量 ②食べること
- **contemporary** 形 同時代の, 現代の
- **contempt** 名 軽蔑, 侮辱, 軽視
- **content** 名 中身, 内容
- **contest** 名 (～を目指す)競争, 競技
- **context** 名 文脈, 前後関係, コンテクスト
- **contiguous** 形 隣接する, 近接する
- **continent** 名 ①大陸, 陸地 ②《the C-》ヨーロッパ大陸 New Continent 新大陸
- **continental** 形 大陸の

- [ ] **continual** 形継続的な, 繰り返される
- [ ] **continually** 副継続的に, 絶えず, ひっきりなしに
- [ ] **contract** 名契約(書), 協定
- [ ] **contradict** 動矛盾する, 否定する, 反論する
- [ ] **contradiction** 名①否定, 反対 ②矛盾
- [ ] **contradictory** 形①矛盾する, 相反する ②議論好きな
- [ ] **contribute** 動①貢献する ②寄稿する ③寄付する
- [ ] **contribution** 名①貢献 ②寄付, 寄贈 ③寄稿, 投稿
- [ ] **control** 動①管理[支配]する ②抑制する, コントロールする 名①管理, 支配(力) ②抑制
- [ ] **controversy** 名論争, 議論
- [ ] **convenient** 形便利な, 好都合な
- [ ] **conventional** 形習慣的な
- [ ] **conversely** 副反対に, 逆に言えば
- [ ] **cooking** 名料理(法), クッキング
- [ ] **cooperate** 動協力する, 一致団結する
- [ ] **cooperation** 名協力, 協業, 協調
- [ ] **copy** 名コピー, 写し 動写す, まねる, コピーする
- [ ] **core** 名核心, 中心, 芯
- [ ] **corn** 名トウモロコシ, 穀物
- [ ] **cornfeed** 名トウモロコシ飼料
- [ ] **corporate** 形団体[共同]の, 会社の
- [ ] **corporation** 名法人, (株式)会社, 公団, 社団法人
- [ ] **corps** 名①軍団, 部隊 ②団体
- [ ] **cost** 名①値段, 費用 ②損失, 犠牲 動(金・費用が)かかる, (〜を)要する, (人に金額を)費やさせる
- [ ] **costly** 形高価な, ぜいたくな, 高くつく
- [ ] **costume** 名衣装, 服装
- [ ] **cottage** 名小別荘, 小さな家
- [ ] **cotton** 名①綿, 綿花 ②綿織物, 綿糸
- [ ] **count** 動①数える ②(〜を…)とみなす ③重要[大切]である **count 〜 as…** (〜を…と)みなす
- [ ] **counter** 動反対[対抗]する, 埋め合わせる **run counter to** 〜に逆行する
- [ ] **counteract** 動打ち消す, 中和する
- [ ] **countless** 形無数の, 数え切れない
- [ ] **countryside** 名地方, 田舎
- [ ] **couple** 名①2つ, 対 ②夫婦, 一組 動つなぐ, つながる, 関連させる
- [ ] **court** 名法廷, 裁判所 **Supreme Court** 最高裁判所
- [ ] **cover** 動①覆う, 包む, 隠す ②扱う, (〜に)わたる, 及ぶ ③代わりを務める ④補う
- [ ] **covered wagon** 幌牛車
- [ ] **cowboy** 名カウボーイ
- [ ] **crack** 名クラック(・コカイン)《煙草で吸引できる状態にしたコカインの塊》
- [ ] **craft** 名①技術, 技巧 ②飛行機
- [ ] **crash** 動①(人・乗り物が)衝突する, 墜落する ②大きな音を立ててぶつかる[壊れる] 名激突, 墜落 **economic crash** 経済恐慌
- [ ] **create** 動創造する, 生み出す, 引き起こす
- [ ] **creator** 名創作者, 創造者, 神
- [ ] **creature** 名(神の)創造物, 生物, 動物
- [ ] **credit** 名①信用, 評判, 名声 ②掛け売り, 信用貸し 動信用する
- [ ] **creditor** 名①債権者, 貸し主 ②貸方《簿記》

America FAQ

- **creed** 名 ①(宗教上の)信条 ②信条, 信念
- **Creole** 名 クレオール人
- **crime** 名 ①(法律上の)罪, 犯罪 ②悪事, よくない行為 **atrocious crime** 凶悪犯罪
- **criminal** 形 犯罪の, 罪深い, 恥ずべき 名 犯罪者, 犯人
- **cripple** 動 だめにする, 破損する
- **crises** 名 crisis (危機) の複数形
- **crisis** 名 ①危機, 難局 ②重大局面 **Cuban Crisis** キューバ危機
- **criticism** 名 批評, 非難, 反論, 評論
- **criticize** 動 ①非難する, あら探しをする ②酷評する ③批評する
- **Cuba** 名 キューバ《国名》
- **Cuban Crisis** キューバ危機
- **Cubism** 名 キュービズム, 立体派《芸術》
- **cultivate** 動 耕す, 栽培する, (才能などを)養う, 育成する
- **cultivation** 名 耕作, 栽培, 育成, 養殖
- **cultivator** 名 耕作者
- **cultural** 形 文化の, 文化的な
- **curb** 動 抑制する, 阻止する, 食い止める
- **currency** 名 ①通貨, 貨幣 ②流通, 通用すること
- **current** 形 現在の, 目下の, 通用[流通]している
- **currently** 副 今のところ, 現在
- **curriculum** 名 履修科目, カリキュラム
- **customary** 形 習慣的な
- **cycle** 名 周期, 循環 **vicious cycle** 悪循環
- **cynical** 形 皮肉な, 冷笑的な, ひねくれた

D

- **Dadaism** 名 ダダイズム《1910年代半ばに起こった芸術思想・芸術運動. 既成の秩序や常識に対する, 否定, 攻撃, 破壊といった思想を大きな特徴とする》
- **Dadaist** 名 ダダイスト《ダダイズムに属する芸術家》
- **daily** 形 毎日の, 日常の
- **dairy** 名 搾乳所, 酪農場, 乳製品販売[製造]所
- **Dallas Cowboys** ダラス・カウボーイズ《テキサス州ダラス都市圏に本拠地を置くプロ・アメリカンフットボール (NFL) チーム》
- **damage** 名 損害, 損傷 動 損害を与える, 損なう
- **Darwin's theory of evolution** ダーウィンの進化論
- **David Dinkins** デイヴィッド・ディンキンズ《アメリカ合衆国の政治家. ニューヨーク市長, 任期1990-1993》
- **day** 熟 **by day** 昼間は, 日中は **day by day** 日ごとに **these days** このごろ **in those days** あのころは, 当時は
- **DEA** 略 麻薬取締局 (Drug Enforcement Administration の略)
- **deadlock** 名 行き詰まり, 膠着(こうちゃく)状態
- **deal** 動 ①分配する ②《–with [in] ~》~を扱う 名 ①取引, 扱い ②(不特定の)量, 額 **a good [great] deal (of ~)** かなり[ずいぶん・大量](の~), 多額(の~)
- **dealer** 名 販売人, ディーラー
- **dealt** 動 deal (分配する) の過去, 過去分詞
- **death** 名 ①死, 死ぬこと ②《the –》終えん, 消滅
- **death row** 死刑囚監房
- **Death Valley** デスヴァレー《カリフォルニア州》

- **debate** 名 討論, ディベート
- **debt** 名 ①借金, 負債 ②恩義, 借り
- **debunk** 動 うそ[偽り]を暴く
- **decade** 名 10年間
- **decay** 名 腐敗, 衰え **urban decay** 都市の衰退
- **decentralized** 形 非集中的, 分散的
- **decision** 名 ①決定, 決心 ②判決
- **decisive** 形 決定的な
- **declaration** 名 ①宣言, 布告 ②告知, 発表
- **Declaration of Independence** アメリカ独立宣言(書)
- **declare** 動 ①宣言する ②断言する ③(税関で)申告する
- **decline** 動 ①断る ②傾く ③衰える 名 ①傾くこと ②下り坂, 衰え, 衰退
- **decrease** 動 減少する 名 減少
- **deep-rooted** 形 根深い
- **deeply** 副 深く, 非常に
- **defeat** 動 ①打ち破る, 負かす ②だめにする 名 ①敗北 ②挫折
- **defend** 動 防ぐ, 守る, 弁護する
- **defendant** 名 被告(人)
- **defense** 名 ①防御, 守備 ②国防 ③弁護, 弁明 **Department of Defense** 国防総省
- **defenseless** 形 無防備の, 防御手段がない
- **deficit** 名 赤字, 不足(額)
- **define** 動 ①定義する, 限定する ②〜の顕著な特性である
- **definitely** 副 ①限定的に, 明確に, 確実に ②まったくそのとおり
- **definitively** 副 決定的に
- **degeneration** 名 退化, 衰退, 変性
- **degree** 名 ①程度, 階級, 位, 身分 ②(温度・角度の)度
- **delegate** 動 権限を委任[委譲]する
- **deleterious effect** 悪影響
- **deliver** 動 ①配達する, 伝える ②達成する, 果たす
- **demand** 動 ①要求する, 尋ねる ②必要とする 名 ①要求, 請求 ②需要
- **democracy** 名 民主主義, 民主政治
- **Democrat** 名 民主党員
- **democratic** 形 ①民主主義の, 民主制の ②民主的な
- **Democratic Party** 民主党
- **demonstrable** 形 実証できる
- **demonstrate** 動 ①デモをする ②実演する ③実証する
- **demonstration** 名 デモ, 示威運動
- **denomination** 名 貨幣単位, 額面金額
- **denote** 動 〜を意味する, 示す
- **deny** 動 否定する, 断る, 受けつけない
- **department** 名 ①部門, 課, 局, 担当分野 ②《D-》(米国・英国の)省
- **Department of Commerce** 米商務省
- **Department of Defense** 国防総省
- **depiction** 名 描写, 表現
- **depression** 名 不景気, 不況 **Great Depression** 世界大恐慌《1929–33年のあいだ世界中の資本主義諸国を襲った史上最大規模の世界恐慌》
- **deprive** 動 奪う, 取り上げる **deprive 〜 of** …から…を奪う
- **derive** 動 ①由来する, 派生する ②(本源から)引き出す ③由来をたどる

America FAQ

- **descendant** 名子孫, 末えい, (祖先からの)伝来物
- **describe** 動 (言葉で)描写する, 特色を述べる, 説明する
- **desert** 名砂漠, 不毛の地
- **design** 動設計する, 企てる 名デザイン, 設計(図)
- **designate** 動 ①示す ②(〜と)称する ③指名する
- **desire** 動強く望む, 欲する 名欲望, 欲求, 願望
- **desperate** 形 ①絶望的な, 見込みのない ②ほしくてたまらない, 必死の
- **despite** 前〜にもかかわらず
- **despotism** 名暴政, 圧政
- **destination** 名行き先, 目的地
- **destroy** 動破壊する, 絶滅させる, 無効にする
- **destruction** 名破壊(行為・状態)
- **detect** 動見つける
- **deteriorate** 動 ①悪化[低下・退廃]する ②悪化させる
- **determination** 名決心, 決定
- **Detroit** 名デトロイト《都市名》
- **devalue** 動 (通貨を)切り下げる
- **devastation** 名荒廃
- **develop** 動 ①発達する[させる] ②開発する
- **development** 名 ①発達, 発展 ②開発
- **device** 名 ①工夫 ②案 ③装置
- **devote** 動 ①(〜を…に)捧げる ②《 – oneself to 〜》〜に専念する
- **differ** 動異なる, 違う, 意見が合わない
- **differential** 名差, 格差
- **digest** 名要約, ダイジェスト Beverage Digest ビバレッジ・ダイジェスト《飲料業界誌》
- **diligence** 名勤勉, たゆまぬ努力
- **diligently** 副勤勉に
- **dime** 名ダイム《10セント硬貨》
- **diplomacy** 名外交, 外交の手腕
- **diplomatic** 形外交(上)の, 外交官の
- **direct** 形まっすぐな, 直接の, 率直な, 露骨な 動 (目・注意・努力などを)向ける
- **direction** 名 ①方向, 方角 ②《-s》指示, 説明書 ③指導, 指揮
- **directly** 副 ①じかに, まっすぐに ②まっすぐ ③ちょうど
- **director** 名管理者, 指導者, 監督
- **disability** 名 ①無力 ②身体障害
- **disadvantage** 名不利な立場[条件], 損失
- **disadvantaged** 形 (経済的・社会的に)恵まれない socially disadvantaged 社会の弱者
- **disagreement** 名 (意見の)不一致, 相違, 不適合
- **disappear** 動見えなくなる, 姿を消す, なくなる
- **disapprove** 動《 – of 〜》〜に不賛成である, 〜に不満[難色]を示す
- **disband** 動 (組織を)解散する, 解体する
- **discard** 動捨てる, 放棄[遺棄]する
- **discipline** 名規律, しつけ
- **discomfort** 名不快(なこと), 辛苦, つらさ
- **discord** 名不一致, 不調和
- **discretion** 名 ①思慮, 分別, 慎重(な姿勢) ②判断[行動]の自由, 裁量
- **discriminate** 動 ①見分ける, 識別する, 区別する ②差別する
- **discrimination** 名差別, 区別, 識別
- **discuss** 動議論[検討]する
- **discussion** 名討議, 討論

WORD LIST

- **disease** 名 ①病気 ②(社会や精神の)不健全な状態
- **dislike** 動嫌う 名反感, いや気
- **dismiss** 動 ①解散する ②解雇する ③捨てる ④却下する
- **dismissal** 名 ①解放, 放免, 解雇 ②(告訴などの)却下
- **Disney** 名ディズニー
- **disorder** 名混乱, 無秩序, 乱雑 動乱す
- **disorientation** 名方向感覚を失うこと
- **disparity** 名格差
- **dispatch** 動発送する, 派遣する, さっさと片づける 名派遣, 急送
- **dispersed** 形分散した
- **display** 動展示する, 示す 名展示, 陳列, 表出
- **disposition** 名 ①気質, 気持ち ②配置, 配列
- **dispute** 名論争, 議論 動反論する, 論争する
- **dissatisfaction** 名不満, 不平
- **dissatisfied** 動 dissatisfy (不満を抱かせる)の過去, 過去分詞 形不満の, 不満そうな
- **distance** 名距離, 隔たり, 遠方
- **distant** 形 ①遠い, 隔たった ②よそよそしい, 距離のある
- **distinct** 形 ①独特な ②はっきりした
- **distinctive** 形独特の, 特色[特徴]のある
- **distribute** 動 ①分配[配布]する ②流通させる
- **distribution** 名 ①分配 ②配布, 配給 ③流通 ④分布, 区分
- **distributor** 名配給業者, 卸業者, 販売業者
- **distrust** 名不信, 疑惑 動疑う, 不信感を抱く
- **disturbance** 名 ①乱すこと, 妨害(物), じゃま ②動揺, 不安
- **diverse** 形 ①種々の, 多様な ②異なった
- **diversify** 動多様化する, 多角化する
- **diversity** 名多様性, 相違
- **divide** 動分かれる, 分ける, 割れる, 割る divide into ~に分かれる be divided into 分けられる
- **division** 名 ①分割 ②部門 ③境界 ④割り算
- **divorce** 動離婚する 名離婚, 分離
- **divorced** 形離婚した
- **doctrinal** 形教義上の
- **doctrine** 名 ①教義, 信条, 主義 ②政策 ③原理, 学説 Monroe Doctrine モンロー主義《欧州諸国による米大陸への干渉を拒否する宣言》
- **dolphin** 名イルカ
- **domestic** 形 ①家庭の ②国内の, 自国の, 国産の
- **dominate** 動支配する, 統治する, 優位を占める
- **Donald Duck** ドナルドダック
- **donate** 動寄付する, 贈与する
- **donkey** 名ロバ
- **dot** 名 ①点, 小数点 ②水玉(模様)
- **dot-com** 名ドットコム企業
- **doubt** 名 ①疑い, 不確かなこと ②未解決点, 困難 no doubt きっと, たぶん 動疑う
- **Douglas Coupland** ダグラス・クープランド《カナダの小説家, 劇作家, 美術家, 1961–》
- **download** 動ダウンロードする
- **downtown** 名街の中心, 繁華街
- **downtrend** 名(景気などの)下降
- **drag** 動 ①引きずる ②のろのろ動く[動かす]
- **drama** 名劇, 演劇, ドラマ, 劇的な

173

AMERICA FAQ

事件

- **dramatically** 副 劇的に, 芝居がかったしぐさで
- **drastic** 形 強烈な, 徹底した
- **draw** 動 ①引く, 引っ張る ②描く ③引き分けになる[する]
- **drawing** 動 draw (引く)の現在分詞
- **drawn** 動 draw (引く)の過去分詞
- **dream of** ～を夢見る
- **drew** 動 draw (引く)の過去
- **drifter** 名 放浪者, 流れ者
- **drive-in** 形 ドライブイン式の
- **drive-through** 形 車に乗ったまま行える, ドライブスルー(式)の
- **driven** 動 drive (車で行く)の過去分詞
- **driver** 名 ①運転手 ②(馬車の)御者
- **drought** 名 ひでり, かんばつ
- **drove** 動 drive (車で行く)の過去
- **drug** 名 薬, 麻薬, 麻酔薬
- **Drug Enforcement Administration** 麻薬取締局
- **drug-related** 形 麻薬がらみの
- **dual-parent** 形 両親の揃った
- **due** 形 予定された, 期日のきている, 支払われるべき **due to** ～によって, ～が原因で
- **duration** 名 持続[継続]期間
- **dust** 名 ちり, ほこり, ごみ, 粉
- **Dutch** 形 オランダの 名 オランダ人の
- **duty** 名 ①義務(感), 責任 ②職務, 任務, 関税
- **Dvorak** 名 (アントニン・)ドヴォルザーク《チェコの作曲家, 1841–1904》
- **dynamic** 形 活動的な, 動的な, ダイナミックな
- **dynamo** 名 発電機

- **dynasty** 名 王朝[王家](の統治期間) **Louis Dynasty** ルイ王朝

E

- **earn** 動 ①儲ける, 稼ぐ ②(名声を)博す
- **earner** 名 稼ぐ人, 稼ぎ手
- **earthquake** 名 地震, 大変動
- **easily** 副 ①容易に, たやすく, 苦もなく ②気楽に
- **East Coast** イースト・コースト, 東海岸
- **eastern** 形 ①東方の, 東向きの ②東洋の, 東洋風の
- **Eastern Europe** 東欧, 東ヨーロッパ
- **easternmost** 形 最も東の, 極東の
- **eco-friendly** 形 環境に優しい[配慮した]
- **economic** 形 経済学の, 経済上の **economic crash** 経済恐慌
- **economic-based** 形 経済に基づく
- **economical** 形 ①経済的な ②倹約する, むだ使いしない
- **economically** 副 経済的に, 節約して
- **economy** 名 ①経済, 財政 ②節約
- **edge** 名 ①刃 ②端, 縁
- **educate** 動 教育する, (～するように)訓練する
- **education** 名 教育, 教養
- **educational** 形 教育(上)の
- **effect** 名 影響, 効果, 結果 **deleterious effect** 悪影響
- **effective** 形 効果的である, 有効である
- **efficiency** 名 ①能率, 効率 ②能力

WORD LIST

- **efficient** 形 ①効率的な, 有効な ②有能な, 敏腕な
- **effort** 名 努力(の成果)
- **egregious** 形 実にひどい, とんでもない
- **Egypt** 名 エジプト《国名》
- **eighteenth** 名 第18番目(の人[もの]), 18日 形 第18番目の
- **either** 熟 on either side 両側に
- **elect** 動 選ぶ, (〜することに)決める, 選挙する
- **election** 名 選挙, 投票
- **elector** 名 選挙人
- **electoral** 形 選挙の
- **electrical** 形 電気の, 電気に関する
- **electricity** 名 電気
- **electronics** 名 エレクトロニクス, 電子工学, 電子機器
- **element** 名 要素, 成分, 元素
- **elementary** 形 ①初歩の ②単純な, 簡単な
- **Elvis Presley** エルヴィス・プレスリー《アメリカのロックンロールミュージシャン, 1935-1977》
- **emancipation** 名 (奴隷の身分・束縛などからの)解放, 釈放
- **embark** 動 乗船する, 着手する, 始める
- **embodiment** 名 具体化, 具現
- **embody** 動 具体化する, 具体的に表現する
- **embroiled in** 〜に巻き込まれる
- **emerge** 動 現れる, 浮かび上がる, 明らかになる
- **emergence** 名 出現, 参入
- **emergency** 名 非常時, 緊急時
- **emigrate** 動 移住する
- **emotion** 名 感激, 感動, 感情
- **emotional** 形 ①感情の, 心理的な ②感情的な, 感激しやすい
- **emphasis** 名 強調, 強勢, 重要性
- **emphasize** 動 ①強調する ②重視する
- **employ** 動 ①(人を)雇う, 使う ②利用する
- **employee** 名 従業員, 会社員, 被雇用者
- **employer** 名 雇主, 使用[利用]する人
- **employment** 名 ①雇用 ②仕事, 職
- **enact** 動 制定する
- **encourage** 動 (〜するように)勧める
- **encouragement** 名 激励, 励み, 促進
- **end** 熟 at the end of 〜の終わりに
- **endangered** 形 危険にさらされた
- **endow** 動 寄付する, 授ける, 寄与する
- **endure** 動 ①我慢する, 耐え忍ぶ ②持ちこたえる
- **enforce** 動 (法律などを)実行する, 実施する, 施行する
- **enforcement** 名 (法律などの)施行, 執行
- **engage** 動 ①約束する, 婚約する ②雇う, 従事する[させる], 《be -d in》〜に従事している
- **engaged in** 〜に従事している, 〜に携わっている
- **engine** 名 エンジン, 機関, (精巧な)機械装置
- **engineer** 名 技師
- **England** 名 ①イングランド ②英国
- **engulf** 動 包み込む, 巻き込む
- **enormous** 形 ばく大な, 非常に大きい, 巨大な
- **enrich** 動 豊かにする, 充実させる
- **enrollment** 名 入学

175

America FAQ

- **ensuing** 形次の, その後の
- **ensure** 動確実にする, 保証する
- **enterprise** 名①企業, 事業 ②計画, 活動
- **entertainment** 名①楽しみ, 娯楽 ②もてなし, 歓待
- **enthusiasm** 名情熱, 熱意, 熱心
- **enthusiastic** 形熱狂的な, 熱烈な
- **entire** 形全体の, 完全な, まったくの
- **entirely** 副完全に, まったく
- **entrepreneur** 名企業家, 起業家
- **environment** 名①環境 ②周囲(の状況), 情勢
- **environment-related** 形環境関連の
- **environmental** 形①環境の, 周囲の ②環境保護の
- **environs** 名近郊, 周辺地域
- **epidemic** 名伝染病, 疫病
- **epithet** 名あだ名, 別称, 形容語句
- **epitome** 名典型(的な例)
- **equal** 形等しい, 均等な, 平等な 動匹敵する, 等しい 名同等のもの[人]
- **equality** 名平等, 等しいこと
- **equally** 副等しく, 平等に
- **equipment** 名装置, 機材, 道具, 設備
- **era** 名時代, 年代
- **Erie** 名エリー湖
- **erupt** 動(火山が)噴火する, 噴出する, 爆発する, (戦争が)勃発する
- **escape** 動逃げる, 免れる, もれる
- **espionage** 名スパイ, 諜報
- **essence** 名①本質, 真髄, 最重要点 ②エッセンス, エキス
- **essentially** 副本質的に, 原則的に, 本来

- **establish** 動確立する, 立証する, 設置[設立]する
- **establishment** 名確立, 設立, 発足
- **estimate** 動①見積もる ②評価する
- **etc.** 略〜など, その他(=et cetera)
- **ethic** 名倫理, 道徳
- **Ethiopian** 名エチオピア人
- **ethnic** 形民族の, 人種的な, エスニックな
- **Europe** 名ヨーロッパ
- **European** 名ヨーロッパ人 形ヨーロッパ(人)の
- **evacuation** 名避難, 疎開
- **evaluation** 名評価
- **evangelist** 名伝道者
- **eve** 名前日, 前夜
- **even if** たとえ〜でも
- **even though** 〜であるけれども, 〜にもかかわらず
- **events** 熟 at all events ともかく, いずれにしても
- **eventually** 副結局は
- **ever more** これまで以上に
- **ever since** それ以来ずっと
- **everybody** 代誰でも, 皆
- **everyday** 形毎日の, 日々の
- **everything** 代すべてのこと[もの], 何でも, 何もかも
- **everywhere** 副どこにいても, いたるところに
- **evidence** 名①証拠, 証人 ②形跡
- **evident** 形明白な, 明らかな
- **evoke** 動(感情などを)呼び起こす, 喚起する, (笑いなどを)誘う
- **evolution** 名①進化 ②展開, 旋回 ③(熱などの)発生 Darwin's theory of evolution ダーウィンの進化論

Word List

- **ex-whaler** 名 元捕鯨(船)員
- **exacerbate** 動 〜を悪化させる
- **exceed** 動 (程度・限度などを)超える, 上回る, 勝る
- **except** 前 〜を除いて, 〜のほかは 接 〜ということを除いて
- **excess** 形 超過の, 過剰な, 余分の
- **excessive** 形 度を超えた, 行き過ぎた, 極端な
- **excitement** 名 興奮(すること)
- **exciting** 形 興奮させる, わくわくさせる
- **execute** 動 ①実行する, 執行する ②死刑にする
- **executive** 名 ①高官, 実行委員 ②重役, 役員, 幹部
- **exempt** 形 免除された
- **exercise** 動 影響を及ぼす
- **exert** 動 ①(力・知力・能力を)出す, 発揮する ②(権力を)行使する
- **exile** 名 追放(者), 亡命(者)
- **exist** 動 存在する, 生存する, ある, いる
- **existence** 名 存在, 実在, 生存
- **existing** 形 現存の, 現在の, 現行の
- **exodus** 名 ①集団での大移動 ②《the E-》(イスラエル人の)エジプト脱出
- **expand** 動 ①広げる, 拡張[拡大]する ②発展させる, 拡充する
- **expectancy** 名 期待, 見込み
- **expelled** 形 (家や土地を)追われた
- **expenditure** 名 ①支出(額), 支払い, 経費, 費用 ②(国家の)歳出, 支出
- **expense** 名 ①出費, 費用 ②犠牲, 代価 **at the expense of** 〜を犠牲にして
- **explore** 動 探検[調査]する, 切り開く

- **explorer** 名 探検者[家]
- **export** 動 輸出する 名 輸出, 国外への持ち出し
- **express** 動 表現する, 述べる
- **expression** 名 ①表現, 表示, 表情 ②言い回し, 語句
- **extend** 動 ①伸ばす, 延長[延期]する ②(範囲が)およぶ, 広がる, (期間などが)渡る
- **extension** 名 ①延長, 伸ばすこと, 継続 ②内線
- **extensive** 形 広い, 広範囲に渡る, 大規模な
- **extenuating circumstances** 酌量すべき事情[状況]
- **extol** 動 褒めそやす, 激賞する
- **extraordinary** 形 異常な, 並はずれた, 驚くべき
- **extreme** 形 極端な, 極度の, いちばん端の
- **extremely** 副 非常に, 極度に
- **exuberantly** 副 生き生きと
- **eye to eye** 目と目が合う

F

- **fabric** 名 ①織物, 生地 ②構造
- **facility** 名 ①《-ties》施設, 設備 ②器用さ, 容易さ
- **fact** 熟 **as a matter of fact** 実際は, 実のところ **in fact** つまり, 実は, 要するに
- **factor** 名 要因, 要素, 因子
- **fail** 動 ①失敗する, 落第する[させる] ②《– to 〜》〜し損なう, 〜できない ③失望させる
- **failure** 名 ①失敗, 落第 ②不足, 欠乏 ③停止, 減退
- **fair** 形 正しい, 公平[正当]な
- **faith** 名 ①信念, 信仰 ②信頼, 信用
- **famine** 名 飢え, 飢饉, 凶作

America FAQ

- ☐ **fantasy** 名空想, 夢想
- ☐ **far** 熟 **as far as** ～と同じくらい遠く, ～まで, ～する限り(では) **how far** どのくらいの距離ですか
- ☐ **farmer** 名農民, 農場経営者
- ☐ **farming** 名農業, 農作業
- ☐ **farmland** 名農地
- ☐ **farther** 副もっと遠く, さらに先に 形もっと向こうの, さらに進んだ
- ☐ **fashion** 名①流行, 方法, はやり ②流行のもの(特に服装)
- ☐ **fast-food** 形ファーストフード専門の, 即席の
- ☐ **fatality** 名①死, 災害, 死者 ②宿命, 致命的なこと
- ☐ **fault** 名断層 **San Andreas fault** サンアンドレアス断層
- ☐ **fauna** 名動物相《特定の地域と年代における動物の総体を表す》
- ☐ **favorably** 副好意的に, 都合よく, 賛成して
- ☐ **FBI** 略連邦捜査局《正式名称Federal Bureau of Investigation, 米国内の複数の州にまたがる犯罪の捜査, 公安情報の収集を任務とする司法省の捜査部門》
- ☐ **fear** 名①恐れ ②心配, 不安 動①恐れる ②心配する
- ☐ **feast** 名①饗宴, ごちそう ②(宗教上の)祝祭日 ③大きな楽しみ
- ☐ **feature** 名①特徴, 特色 ②顔の一部, 《-s》顔立ち ③(ラジオ・テレビ・新聞などの)特集
- ☐ **federal** 形連邦政府の, 連邦の
- ☐ **Federal Bureau of Investigation** 連邦捜査局《略称FBI, 米国内の複数の州にまたがる犯罪の捜査, 公安情報の収集を任務とする司法省の捜査部門》
- ☐ **Federal Reserve Bank** 連邦準備銀行
- ☐ **Federal Reserve note** 連邦準備券

- ☐ **federalist** 名連邦党(1787年に結成されたアメリカの政党)支持者
- ☐ **fertile** 形①肥沃な ②繁殖力のある ③創造力に富む
- ☐ **fertilizer** 名①(化学)肥料 ②豊かにする人[物] ③受精媒介者
- ☐ **fetter** 名足枷
- ☐ **fierce** 形どう猛な, 荒々しい, すさまじい, 猛烈な
- ☐ **fiftieth** 形①《the –》50番目の ②50分の1の 名①《the –》50番目 ②50分の1
- ☐ **fight** 熟 **fight with** ～と戦う **put up a fight** 抵抗する, 戦う
- ☐ **figure out** 理解する, ～であるとわかる, (原因などを)解明する
- ☐ **file a protest with** ～に抗議を申し込む
- ☐ **file a tax return** 確定申告をする
- ☐ **film** 名フィルム, 映画
- ☐ **filmmaker** 名映画制作者[会社]
- ☐ **final** 形最後の, 決定的な 名①最後のもの ②期末[最終]試験 ③《-s》決勝戦
- ☐ **finance** 名①財政, 財務 ②(銀行からの)資金, 融資 ③《-s》財政状態, 財源
- ☐ **finance-related** 形金融関係の
- ☐ **financial** 形①財務(上)の, 財政(上)の, 金融(上)の ②金融関係者の
- ☐ **firework** 名花火
- ☐ **firm** 形堅い, しっかりした, 断固とした 名会社, 事務所
- ☐ **first of all** まず第一に
- ☐ **first-generation** 形外国移民の子としてアメリカで生まれた, 二世の
- ☐ **fishermen** 名漁師《fishermanの複数形》
- ☐ **fix** 動①固定する[させる] ②修理する ③決定する ④用意する, 整える
- ☐ **fixed** 形固定した, ゆるぎない

WORD LIST

- **flash** 名（カメラの）フラッシュ
- **fled** 動 flee（逃げる）の過去, 過去分詞
- **flee** 動 逃げる, 逃亡する
- **flesh** 名 肉
- **floating** 形 流動的な
- **flood** 名 ①洪水 ②殺到
- **flora** 名 植物相《特定の地域と年代における植物の総体を表す》
- **Florida** 名 フロリダ州
- **flourish** 動 繁栄する, 栄える
- **flow** 動 流れ出る, 流れる, あふれる 名 ①流出 ②流ちょう（なこと）
- **fluctuate** 形（不規則に）変動する
- **flutter** 動 はためく
- **fog** 名 濃霧, 煙
- **folk** 形 民間の, 民衆の
- **folk-music** 形 民族音楽の
- **follower** 名 信奉者, 追随者
- **following** 形《the-》次の, 次に続く 名《the-》下記のもの, 以下に述べるもの
- **foot** 熟 on foot 歩いて
- **football** 名（英国で）サッカー,（米国で）アメリカンフットボール
- **footprint** 名 足型, 足跡 carbon footprint 二酸化炭素排出量
- **for a while** しばらくの間, 少しの間
- **force** 名 力, 勢い 動 ①強制する, 力ずくで～する, 余儀なく～させる ②押しやる, 押し込む
- **Ford** 形 フォード《社名》
- **forecast** 動 ①予見する ②前もって計画をたてる, 予定する ③予測する, 予報する
- **forefather** 名（男の）祖先, 先祖
- **forefront** 名 最前部, 最前線, 第一線
- **foremost** 形 真っ先の, 第一の 副 真っ先に, 第一に
- **foreseeable** 形 予測［予知］できる
- **foreseen** 動 foresee（予見する）の過去分詞
- **form** 名 ①形, 形式 ②書式 composite art form 総合芸術様式 動 形づくる
- **format** 名 フォーマット, 形式
- **formation** 名 ①形成, 編成 ②隊形, フォーメーション
- **formative** 形 ①造形の, 形成の, 発達の ②語形成に用いる, 成語的な
- **former** 形 ①前の, 先の, 以前の ②《the-》（二者のうち）前者の
- **forth** 副 前へ, 外へ and so forth など, その他
- **forty-niners** 名 1849年のゴールドラッシュにカリフォルニアにやって来た人たちのこと
- **foster** 動 ①育てる, 促進させる ②心に抱く
- **found** 動 ～を設立する, 創立する
- **foundation** 名 ①建設, 創設 ②基礎, 土台
- **founding** 形 設立の, 創立の
- **framework** 名 骨組み, 構造, 組織
- **France** 名 フランス《国名》
- **Francis Scott Key** フランシス・スコット・キー《アメリカ合衆国の国歌である "The Star-Spangled Banner"（星条旗）の歌詞を書いたアマチュアの詩人, 1779–1843》
- **Franklin Delano Roosevelt** フランクリン・デラノ・ルーズベルト《アメリカ合衆国の政治家, 第32代アメリカ大統領, 任期1933–1945》
- **frantically** 副 取り乱して, 半狂乱で
- **freedom** 名 ①自由 ②束縛がないこと
- **freely** 副 自由に, 障害なしに
- **freeway** 名 高速道路

179

America FAQ

- **freight** 名 貨物輸送, 運送貨物
- **French** 形 フランス(人・語)の 名 ①フランス語 ②《the –》フランス人
- **French and Indian Wars** フレンチ・インディアン戦争《北アメリカ植民地で行われたフランス・インディアンの連合軍とイギリスとの戦争, 1755–1763》
- **frequent** 形 ひんぱんな, よくある
- **frequently** 副 頻繁に, しばしば
- **fresh-water lake** 淡水湖
- **friction** 名 摩擦, 不和
- **friend** 熟 make friends with ～と友達になる
- **friendly** 形 親しみのある, 親切な, 友情のこもった 副 友好的に, 親切に
- **from ～ onwards** ～以降
- **from time to time** ときどき
- **frontier** 名 ①国境, 辺境, フロンティア ②〈-s〉最先端
- **fry** 名 揚げ物, いため物
- **fuel** 名 燃料
- **full-scale** 形 全面的な, 完全な
- **function** 動 働く, 機能する 名 機能, 作用
- **fund** 名 ①資金, 基金, 財源 ②金 ③公債, 国債
- **fundamental** 形 基本の, 根本的な, 重要な
- **fundamentalist** 名 原理主義者の
- **funding** 名 ①財源 ②財政支援 ③資金調達
- **fur** 名 毛, 毛皮(製品)
- **furious** 形 怒り狂った, 激怒した, 激しい
- **further** 形 いっそう遠い, その上の, なおいっそうの 副 いっそう遠く, その上に, もっと 動 促進する
- **furthermore** 副 さらに, その上
- **future** 熟 in the future 将来は
- **futuristic** 形 革新的な

G

- **gain** 動 ①得る, 増す ②進歩する, 進む
- **gain access to** に近づく, に接近する
- **gallery** 名 美術館, 画廊, 回廊, 観客
- **Galveston** 名 ガルベストン《地名》
- **gambling** 名 賭博
- **gang** 名 ギャング, 暴力団
- **gap** 名 ギャップ, 隔たり, すき間
- **gather** 動 ①集まる, 集める ②生じる, 増す ③推測する
- **gay** 形 同性愛の 名 同性愛者
- **GDP** 略 国内総生産
- **gender** 名 (社会的に決められた)性, 性別
- **general** 形 ①全体の, 一般の, 普通の ②おおよその ③(職位の)高い, 上級の general store 雑貨屋 general public 一般公衆 名 大将, 将軍
- **General Motors** ゼネラル・モーターズ《社名》
- **generalized** 形 汎用の
- **generally** 副 ①一般に, だいたい ②たいてい
- **generate** 動 生み出す, 引き起こす
- **generation** 名 ①同世代の人々 ②一世代 ②発生, 生成
- **Generation X** ジェネレーションX《第二次大戦後のベビーブームの後に生まれた将来の展望を欠いた無気力な世代》
- **Generation Xers** ジェネレーションX世代の人々

180

- **gentle** 形 ①優しい, 温和な ②柔らかな
- **gently** 副 親切に, 上品に, そっと, 優しく
- **geographical** 形 地理的な, 地理学上の
- **geographically** 副 地理的に
- **geologically** 副 地質学的に
- **George Gershwin** ジョージ・ガーシュウィン《アメリカの作曲家, 1898–1937》
- **George W. Bush** ジョージ・W・ブッシュ《アメリカ合衆国の政治家。第43代アメリカ合衆国大統領, 任期 2001–2009》
- **George Washington** ジョージ・ワシントン《アメリカ合衆国の軍人, 政治家, 初代大統領, 任期 1789–1797》
- **Georgia** 名 ジョージア州
- **germ** 名 ①細菌, 病原菌 ②胚 ③萌芽
- **German** 形 ドイツ(人・語)の 名 ①ドイツ人 ②ドイツ語
- **Germany** 名 ドイツ《国名》
- **get away** 逃げる, 逃亡する, 離れる
- **get caught** 逮捕される
- **get into** ~に入る, 入り込む, ~に巻き込まれる
- **ghost** 名 幽霊
- **giant** 名 ①巨人, 大男 ②巨匠 形 巨大な, 偉大な
- **gigantic** 形 巨大な, 膨大な
- **give rise to** ~を引き起こす
- **glittering** 形 光り輝く, きらびやかな
- **global** 形 地球(上)の, 地球規模の, 世界的な, 国際的な
- **global warming** 地球温暖化
- **globally** 副 全世界的に
- **globe** 名 ①球 ②地球
- **glory** 名 栄光, 名誉, 繁栄
- **glow** 名 ①白熱, 輝き ②ほてり, 熱情
- **glowing** 形 白熱[赤熱]した, 熱のこもった
- **gnaw** 動 かじる, むしばむ, 苦しめる
- **go** 熟 **go all the way** ずっと, 完全に, 行くところまで行く **go bankrupt** 破産する **go on to** ~に移る, ~に取り掛かる **go out** 外出する, 外へ出る **go straight on** 一直線に進む **go up** ①~に上がる, 登る ②~に近づく, 出かける ③(建物などが)建つ, 立つ **go with** ~と一緒に行く, ~と調和する, ~にとても似合う
- **goblin** 名 ゴブリン, 小鬼
- **God** 名 神
- **gold** 名 金, 金貨, 金製品, 金色
- **Gold Rush** ゴールドラッシュ《カリフォルニアのサクラメントの近くで1848年に金鉱が発見され, 世界中から一攫千金を夢見るおびただしい移民が殺到した, 1848–1855》
- **golden** 形 ①金色の ②金製の ③貴重な
- **Golden Gate Bridge** ゴールデン・ゲート・ブリッジ
- **Gone with the Wind** 風と共に去りぬ《映画, 1939》
- **goods** 名 ①商品, 品物 ②財産, 所有物
- **Google** 名 グーグル
- **government** 名 政治, 政府, 支配
- **governor** 名 ①知事 ②支配者, (学校・病院・官庁などの)長
- **gradually** 副 だんだんと
- **graduate** 名 卒業生
- **granary** 名 穀倉地帯, 穀物倉
- **grand** 形 雄大な, 壮麗な
- **Grand Canyon** グランドキャニオン

America FAQ

- **grant** 動 ①許可する, 承諾する ② 授与する, 譲渡する
- **grasp** 動 つかむ, 握る, とらえる, 理解する
- **grass** 草, 牧草(地)
- **Great Britain** 大ブリテン島《英国の主島》
- **Great Depression** 世界大恐慌《1929–33年のあいだ世界中の資本主義諸国を襲った史上最大規模の世界恐慌》
- **Great Lakes** 五大湖
- **greatly** 副 大いに
- **Greek** 形 ギリシャ(人・語)の 名 ①ギリシャ人 ②ギリシャ語
- **Green Party** 緑の党
- **greenery** 名 青葉, 緑の木
- **grow into** 成長して〜になる
- **grow to** 〜するようになる
- **grow up** 成長する, 大人になる
- **growth** 名 成長, 発展 形 成長している
- **Guam** 名 グアム島
- **Guantanamo military base** グァンタナモ米軍基地《キューバ東南部のグァンタナモ湾に位置するアメリカ海軍の基地》
- **guarantee** 名 保証, 保証書, 保証人 動 保証する, 請け合う
- **guaranteed** 形 保証された, 保証付きの
- **guest** 名 客, ゲスト
- **Guggenheim** 名 グッゲンハイム《ユダヤ系ドイツ人の家系で, アメリカに移民したマイアー・グッゲンハイムとその子供たち。鉱山の経営と精錬で大成功し財を成し, 後に近代美術への支援などの慈善活動を行った》
- **guilty** 形 有罪の, やましい
- **Gulf of Mexico** メキシコ湾
- **gun** 名 銃, 大砲
- **gun-seller** 名 銃砲店
- **gunfire** 名 発砲

H

- **hall** 名 公会堂, ホール, 大広間, 玄関
- **Halloween** 名 ハロウィーン《万聖節の前夜。10月31日》
- **hamburger** 名 ハンバーガー
- **hand** 熟 hand in 差し出す, 提出する on the other hand 一方, 他方では
- **handle** 動 取り扱う
- **hang around** うろつく
- **Hanukkah** 名 ハヌカー《ユダヤ教の清めの祭り》
- **happiness** 名 幸せ, 喜び
- **harass** 動 悩ます, 苦しめる, いやがらせる sexually harass セクハラ[性的嫌がらせ]をする
- **harassment** 名 いやがらせ, ハラスメント
- **harbor** 名 港, 停泊所 Pearl Harbor パールハーバー, 真珠湾《地名》
- **hardship** 名 (耐えがたい)苦難, 辛苦
- **hardworking** 形 勤勉な, よく働く
- **Harper's Index** ハーパーズ・インデックス《ハーパー誌の人気コーナー, 政治情勢を統計と独自のデータで紹介している》
- **Harry S. Truman** ハリー・S・トルーマン《アメリカ合衆国の第34代副大統領および第33代大統領, 任期(大統領)1945–1953》
- **harsh** 形 厳しい, とげとげしい, 不快な
- **harvest** 名 収穫, 刈り入れ
- **hastily** 副 急いで, 軽率に
- **hate** 動 嫌う, 憎む, (〜するのを)いやがる 名 憎しみ

Word List

- **hatred** 名憎しみ, 毛嫌い
- **haunt** 動よく行く, 出没する, つきまとう
- **have something made** ～を作らせる
- **haves and have-nots** 持てる者と持たざる者
- **Hawaii** 名ハワイ《米国の州》
- **head of** ～の長
- **headache** 名頭痛
- **headquarters** 名本部, 司令部, 本署
- **health care** 健康保険制度
- **healthcare** 名(医療機関を通じた)ヘルス・ケア, 健康管理
- **heap** 名(積み重ねた)山, かたまり
- **Heartland** 名(アメリカの)中部地域, ハートランド
- **heat** 名①熱, 暑さ ②熱気, 熱意, 激情
- **heaven** 名①天国 ②天国のようなところ[状態], 楽園 ③空 ④〈H-〉神
- **heavy lift rocket** 重量物打ち上げロケット
- **heed** 名注意 take heed of ～に留意する
- **heighten** 動①強める, 高じさせる ②～を高くする
- **herder** 名家畜の世話をする人
- **heresy** 名異端
- **hesitate** 動ためらう, ちゅうちょする
- **hi-tech** 形ハイテクな[の]
- **hide** 動隠れる, 隠す, 隠れて見えない, 秘密にする
- **high-tech** 名ハイテク, 高度[先端]技術
- **highlight** 動注目させる, 強調する
- **highly** 副①大いに, 非常に ②高度に, 高位に ③高く評価して, 高価で
- **hijack** 動①ハイジャックする, 乗っ取る ②襲って盗む
- **hint** 名暗示, ヒント, 気配
- **hippie** 名ヒッピー
- **Hispanic** 名ラテンアメリカ系の人, スペイン語を話す人 形ラテンアメリカ系の, スペイン(人, 語)の
- **historical** 形歴史の, 歴史上の, 史実に基づく
- **historically** 副歴史的に
- **hockey** 名(スポーツの)ホッケー
- **holed up** 《be－》立てこもっている
- **holiday** 名 national holiday 国民の休日
- **Holland** 名オランダ《国》
- **Hollywood** 名ハリウッド《地名》
- **holy** 形聖なる, 神聖な
- **homeless** 形家のない, ホームレスの
- **homosexual** 形同性愛の
- **homosexuality** 名同性愛
- **honest** 形①正直な, 誠実な, 心からの ②公正な, 感心な
- **Hong Kong** 香港
- **honk** 動(クラクションを)鳴らす
- **honor** 動尊敬する, 栄誉を与える
- **hopelessly** 副希望を失って, どうしようもなく
- **hospitality** 名歓待, 温かいもてなし Southern Hospitality 米国南部の温かいもてなし
- **hostilities** 名戦闘
- **House of Representatives** 下院
- **household** 形家族の
- **housing loan** 住宅ローン
- **Houston** 名ヒューストン《地名》
- **how far** どのくらいの距離ですか

America FAQ

- **however** 副たとえ～でも 接けれども, だが
- **hub** 名中心地, 拠点
- **Hudson River group** ハドソン・リバー派《ロマン派の影響を受けた風景画家のグループによる, 19世紀中頃のアメリカの美術運動》
- **huge** 形巨大な, ばく大な
- **human being** 人, 人間
- **hunting** 名狩り, 狩猟, ハンティング
- **Huron** 名ヒューロン湖
- **hurricane** 名ハリケーン
- **Hurricane Katrina** ハリケーン・カトリーナ《2005年8月末にアメリカ合衆国南東部を襲った大型のハリケーン》
- **hysterical** 形ヒステリックな, ヒステリー症の

I

- **Ice Age** 氷河紀［時代］
- **ice hockey** アイスホッケー
- **Idaho** 名アイダホ州
- **ideal** 名理想, 究極の目標
- **idealize** 動理想化する
- **identify** 動①(本人・同一と)確認する, 見分けする ②意気投合する
- **identity** 名①同一であること ②本人であること ③独自性
- **if** 熟 as if あたかも～のように, まるで～みたいに even if たとえ～でも if any もしあれば, あったとしても if necessary もし必要ならば see if ～かどうかを確かめる
- **ignore** 動無視する, 怠る
- **illegal** 形違法な, 不法な illegal alien 不法入国者
- **Illinois** 名イリノイ州
- **illness** 名病気

- **image** 名①印象, 姿 ②画像, 映像
- **imagination** 名想像(力), 空想
- **imagine** 動想像する, 心に思い描く
- **imbued with** 《be –》染み込んでいる
- **immerse** 動①浸す, 沈める ②没頭させる
- **immigrant** 名移民, 移住者 形移民に関する
- **immigrate** 動(他国から)移住する, 移住させる
- **immigration** 名①移民局, 入国管理 ②移住, 入植
- **impact** 名影響力, 反響, 効果
- **impartial** 形公平な, 偏見のない, 偏りのない
- **impede** 動妨げる, 邪魔をする
- **implement** 動①実行する ②道具［手段］を提供する
- **import** 動輸入する 名輸入, 輸入品
- **impose** 動課す, 負わせる, 押しつける impose on ～につけこむ, ～に押しつける
- **imposing** 形印象的な, 人目をひく, 立派な
- **imposition** 名課すこと, 押しつけること
- **impress** 動印象づける, 感銘させる
- **impressionist** 名印象派の画家
- **imprisonment** 名投獄, 交流 life imprisonment 終身刑
- **improve** 動改善する［させる］, 進歩する
- **improvement** 名改良, 改善
- **inaugurate** 動～を就任させる
- **inauguration** 名就任式, 就任演説
- **incarceration** 名投獄, 監禁

Word List

- **inception** 名 始まり, 開始
- **incident** 名 出来事, 事故, 事変, 紛争
- **incidentally** 副 偶然に
- **include** 動 含む, 勘定に入れる
- **included** 形 含む
- **including** 動 include（含む）の現在分詞 前 ～を含めて, 込みで
- **income** 名 収入, 所得, 収益
- **incorporate** 動 ①合体させる ②法人組織にする
- **incorporation** 名 結合
- **increase** 動 増加［増強］する, 増やす, 増える 名 増加(量), 増大
- **increasing** 形 増えている, 増加の
- **increasingly** 副 ますます, だんだん
- **incredible** 形 ①信じられない, 信用できない ②すばらしい, とてつもない
- **indeed** 副 実際, 本当に
- **independence** 名 独立, 独立心, 自立 Declaration of Independence アメリカ独立宣言（書） War of Independence 独立戦争
- **Independence Day** インディペンデンス・デー,（合衆国）独立記念日
- **independent** 形 独立した, 自立した
- **index** 名 ①索引 ②しるし, 現れ ③指数
- **India** 名 インド《国名》
- **Indian** 名 ①インド人 ②（アメリカ）インディアン 形 ①インド（人）の ②（アメリカ）インディアンの
- **indicate** 動 ①指す, 示す,（道などを）教える ②それとなく言う ③きざしがある
- **indication** 名 ①指示, 暗示するもの ②表示, 指摘

- **indicator** 名 指標, 指針
- **indigenous** 形 原産の, 生まれつきの
- **indirect** 形 間接的な, 二次的な
- **indirectly** 副 間接（的）に, 遠回しに
- **individual** 形 独立した, 個性的な, 個々の 名 個体, 個人
- **individualism** 名 個人主義
- **indomitable** 形 不屈の
- **indoor** 形 室内の, 屋内の
- **indulge** 動 ①満足する［させる］, 甘やかす ②ふける, 従事する
- **industrial** 形 工業の, 産業の
- **industry** 名 産業, 工業
- **industry-leading** 形 業界最高レベルの
- **infant** 名 ①幼児 ②初心者, 入門者
- **infected with**〈be –〉感染する
- **infection** 名（病気など）感染, 伝染
- **inflame** 動 ①怒らせる, あおる ②炎症を起こさせる
- **influence** 名 影響, 勢力 動 影響をおよぼす
- **influential** 形 影響力の大きい, 有力な
- **influx** 名 流入
- **inhabit** 動 ①（ある場所に）住む, 居住する ②～に存在する, 宿る
- **inhabitant** 名 居住者, 住民
- **inherit** 動 相続する, 受け継ぐ
- **initiative** 名 主導権, イニシアチブ
- **injection** 名 ①注入, 注射 ②（資金の）つぎ込み, 投入
- **injure** 動 痛める, 傷つける
- **injured** 形 負傷した
- **inland** 形 ①内陸の, 奥地の ②国内の, 内地の 副 内陸に, 奥地に
- **inner-city slum** 都心のスラム街

America FAQ

- **inquire** 動尋ねる, 問う
- **inroad** 名侵略, 侵害
- **instability** 名不安定(性)
- **instead** 副その代わりに
- **institute** 動①制定する ②(調査を)実施する 名協会, 研究所
- **institution** 名①設立, 制定 ②制度, 慣習 ③協会, 公共団体
- **instruction** 名教えること, 指示, 助言
- **instrument** 名①道具, 器具, 器械 ②楽器 ③手段
- **insufficient** 形①不十分な, 不足して ②不適当な, 能力のない
- **insurance** 名保険
- **integrate** 動①統合する, 一体化する ②溶け込ませる, 溶け込む, 差別をなくす
- **intellectual** 形知的な, 知性のある 名知識人, 有識者
- **intelligence** 名①知能 ②情報
- **intense** 形①強烈な, 激しい ②感情的な
- **intensify** 動強める, 増大する
- **intensive** 形①集中的な, 集中した ②激しい, 強い
- **intent** 形①専念した, 熱心な ②《be ~ on ~》〜するつもりである 名意図, 意向
- **intention** 名①意図, (〜する)つもり ②心構え
- **inter** 動埋葬する
- **interested** 動 interest(興味を起こさせる)の過去, 過去分詞 形興味を持った, 関心のある
- **interestingly** 副面白いことに
- **interference** 名①妨害, 干渉 ②雑音, 電波障害
- **interpret** 動①通訳する ②説明する ③解釈する
- **intersect** 名交差

- **Interstate 80** 州間高速道路80号線《カリフォルニア州サンフランシスコから, ニューヨーク市の郊外にあたるニュージャージー州ティネックまでを結ぶ》
- **intervene** 動①間に入る, 介入する, 干渉する ②仲裁する, 調停する
- **intervention** 名介入, 仲裁, 調停, 干渉
- **introduction** 名紹介, 導入
- **invade** 動侵入する, 攻め入る
- **invaluable** 形とても有益な
- **invasion** 名侵略, 侵害
- **invent** 動①発明[考案]する ②ねつ造する
- **invention** 名①発明(品) ②作り事, でっち上げ
- **invest** 動投資する, (金・精力などを)注ぐ
- **investigation** 名(徹底的な)調査, 取り調べ **Federal Bureau of Investigation** 連邦捜査局《略称FBI, 米国内の複数の州にまたがる犯罪の捜査, 公安情報の収集を任務とする司法省の捜査部門》
- **investment** 名投資, 出資
- **investor** 名①出資者, 投資家 ②授与者
- **involve** 動①含む, 伴う ②巻き込む, かかわらせる
- **involved** 形①巻き込まれている, 関連する ②入り組んだ, 込み入っている
- **involvement** 名関与
- **Iraq** 名イラク《国名》
- **Ireland** 名アイルランド《国名》
- **Irish** 形アイルランド(人)の 名①アイルランド人 ②アイルランド語
- **irony** 名皮肉, 反語, あてこすり
- **Iroquois** 名イルコイ族
- **irresponsible** 形責任感のない
- **irritation** 名①いらだたせること,

186

いらだち, 立腹 ②刺激
- **Islam** 名 イスラム教［教徒・文化］
- **Islamic** 形 イスラムの, イスラム教の
- **isolationism** 名 孤立主義（政策）
- **Israel** 名 イスラエル《国名》
- **issuance** 名 発行, 支給
- **issue** 名 ①問題, 論点 ②発行物 ③出口, 流出 issue of 単一争点の, 一つの問題だけに焦点をしぼった 動 ①（～から）出る, 生じる ②発行する
- **It is ~ for someone to …** （人）が…するのは～だ
- **Italian** 形 イタリア（人・語）の 名 ①イタリア人 ②イタリア語
- **Italy** 名 イタリア《国名》
- **item** 名 ①項目, 品目 ②（新聞などの）記事
- **itself** 代 それ自体, それ自身

J

- **Japanese-Russo War** 日露戦争《日本とロシアの戦争, 1904–05》
- **jazz** 名 ジャズ
- **jeans** 名 ジーンズ, ジーパン
- **Jerusalem** 名 エルサレム《地名》 Temple in Jerusalem エルサレム神殿
- **Jesus Christ** イエス・キリスト
- **Jewish** 形 ユダヤ人の, ユダヤ教の
- **Jewish holy days** ユダヤ教の祝祭日
- **Jewish Power** ユダヤ・パワー
- **John F. Kennedy** ジョン・F・ケネディ《第35代アメリカ合衆国大統領, 任期1961–1963》
- **John Smith** ジョン・スミス《イギリスの軍人, 探検家, ジェームズタウンを建設, またニューイングランドを命名した。1580–1631》
- **John Stafford Smith** ジョン・スタフォード・スミス《イギリスの作曲家, 1931年にアメリカ合衆国国歌「星条旗」になった,「天国のアナクレオンへ」を書いた, 1750–1836》
- **John Wayne** ジョン・ウェイン《アメリカの俳優, 1907–1979》
- **joint** 名 共同の, ジョイントした
- **Joseph Smith** ジョセフ・スミス《末日聖徒イエス・キリスト教会（俗称モルモン教）の設立者, 1805–1844》
- **journey** 名 ①（遠い目的地への）旅 ②行程
- **Judaism** 名 ユダヤ教
- **judge** 判決を下す, 裁く, 判断する, 評価する 名 裁判官, 判事, 審査員
- **judgment** 名 ①判断, 意見 ②裁判, 判決
- **judicial** 形 裁判（官）の, 司法の
- **junior high school** 中学校
- **jurisdiction** 名 裁判権, 司法権
- **juror** 名 陪審員
- **jury** 名 ①陪審, 陪審員団 ②（展示会・競技会などの）審査員団, 調査委員会
- **justice** 名 ①公平, 公正, 正当, 正義 ②司法, 裁判（官）
- **justify** 動 正しいとする, 弁明する
- **juvenile** 形 児童の, 少年［少女］の

K

- **Kansas** 名 カンザス州
- **Kansas City** カンザスシティ《都市名》
- **Katrina** 名 Hurricane Katrina ハリケーン・カトリーナ《2005年8月末にアメリカ合衆国南東部を襲った大型のハリケーン》
- **keep out of** ～を避ける, ～に干渉しない

America FAQ

- **Kennedy**（ジョン・F・）ケネディ《第35代アメリカ合衆国大統領, 任期1961-1963》
- **Kentucky** 名ケンタッキー州
- **km** 名キロメートル《単位》
- **knowledge** 名知識, 理解, 学問
- **known as**《be –》～として知られている
- **known to**《be –》～に知られている
- **Korean** 形韓国(人・語)の, 朝鮮(人・語)の 名①韓国［朝鮮］人 ②韓国［朝鮮］語
- **Korean Peninsula** 朝鮮半島

L

- **LA** 略ロサンゼルス
- **labor** 名労働, 骨折り
- **Labor Day** 労働者の日, レイバー・デー
- **labor union** 労働組合
- **lack** 名不足, 欠乏
- **lag** 動①遅れる ②(興味などが)衰える
- **laden with** ～に苦しんでいる
- **laid** 動lay (置く) の過去, 過去分詞
- **lake** 名 fresh-water lake 淡水湖 Great Lakes 五大湖
- **landscape** 名①景色, 風景 ②見晴らし ③風景画
- **lane** 名車線, 小道
- **lantern** 名手提げランプ, ランタン
- **large** at large 全体として, 広く
- **large-scale** 形大規模の
- **Las Vegas** ラスベガス《地名》
- **last** 熟 at last ついに, とうとう
- **Latin** 名①ラテン語 ②ラテン系民族の人 形ラテン(語・系)の
- **Latino** 形ラテンアメリカ系住民の

- **latter** 形①後の, 末の, 後者の ②《the –》後者《代名詞的に用いる》
- **lawsuit** 名訴訟, 告訴
- **lawyer** 名弁護士, 法律家
- **LAX airport** ロサンゼルス国際空港
- **lay** 動①置く, 横たえる, 敷く ②整える ③卵を産む ④lie (横たわる) の過去
- **lay-off** 名レイオフ, 一時解雇
- **lead into** (ある場所)へ導く
- **lead to** ～に至る, ～に通じる, ～を引き起こす
- **leadership** 名指揮, リーダーシップ
- **leading** 形主要な, 指導的な, 先頭の leading role 主導的役割
- **league** 名①同盟, 連盟 ②(スポーツの) 競技連盟
- **League of Nations** 国際連盟
- **least** 名最小, 最少 at least 少なくとも
- **leave behind** 熟 あとにする, ～を置き去りにする
- **led** 動 lead (導く) の過去, 過去分詞
- **Lee** 名 (ロバート・E・) リー《南北戦争の時代のアメリカの軍人。南部連合の軍司令官を務めた, 1807-1870》
- **legal** 形法律(上)の, 正当な
- **legally** 副合法的に, 法律的に
- **legislative** 形立法上の, 立法機関の
- **legitimacy** 名合法性, 正当性, 嫡出であること
- **Lehman Brothers** リーマン・ブラザーズ《アメリカのニューヨークに本社を置いていた大手投資銀行及び証券会社, 2008年倒産》
- **leisure** 名余暇 形余暇の
- **leisured class** 有閑階級
- **length** 名長さ, 縦, たけ, 距離

188

Word List

- **lent** 動 lend（貸す）の過去, 過去分詞
- **Leonard Bernstein** レナード・バーンスタイン《ユダヤ系アメリカ人の作曲家・指揮者, 1918-1990》
- **less** 形 ～より小さい［少ない］ 副 ～より少なく, ～ほどでなく
- **level** 名 ①水平, 平面 ②水準
- **Levi Strauss** リーヴァイ・ストラウス《ユダヤ系ドイツ人移民の企業家。リーバイ・ストラウス社の創業者のひとり, 1829-1902》
- **Levi's** 名 リーバイス
- **liberate** 動 自由にする, 解放する
- **liberation** 名 ①解放, 釈放 ②解放運動
- **liberty** 名 ①自由, 解放 ②《-ties》特権, 特典 ③《-ties》勝手な振る舞い
- **lid** 名 （箱, なべなどの）ふた
- **lie** 動 （ある状態に）ある, 存在する, 位置する
- **life imprisonment** 終身刑
- **life sentence** 終身刑
- **lifeline** 名 生命線
- **lifestyle** 名 生活様式, ライフスタイル
- **lift** 名 ①持ち上げること ②エレベーター, リフト **heavy lift rocket** 重量物打ち上げロケット
- **likely** 形 ①ありそうな, (～)しそうな ②適当な 副 たぶん, おそらく
- **limit** 名 限界,《-s》範囲, 境界 動 制限［限定］する
- **limitation** 名 制限, 限度
- **limited** 動 limit（制限する）の過去, 過去分詞 形 限られた, 限定の
- **Lincoln** 名 （エイブラハム・）リンカーン《米国第16代大統領, 在任1861-65》
- **list** 名 名簿, 目録, 一覧表
- **literally** 副 文字どおり, そっくりそのまま
- **Little League** リトルリーグ《少年野球連盟》
- **live up to** （理想などに）ふさわしい暮らしをする,（期待などに）そう
- **livestock** 名 家畜
- **living** 名 生計, 生活 **make a living** 生計［暮らし］を立てる 形 ①生きている, 現存の ②使用されている
- **loan** 名 貸付（金）, ローン **housing loan** 住宅ローン 動 貸す
- **lobby** 動 圧力をかける
- **location** 名 位置, 場所
- **logo** 名 ロゴ, 文字, 意匠文字
- **Loma Prieta** ロマ・プリータ地震《1989年10月17日にカリフォルニア州北部で発生した地震》
- **loneliness** 名 孤独
- **lonely** 形 ①孤独な, 心さびしい ②ひっそりした, 人里離れた
- **long** 熟 **as long as** ～する以上は, ～である限りは
- **long-standing** 形 ずっと昔からの, 長年［長期］にわたる
- **longer** 熟 **no longer** もはや～でない［～しない］
- **look for** ～を探す
- **loose** 形 自由な, ゆるんだ, あいまいな 動 ほどく, 解き放つ
- **Los Angelean** ロサンゼルス住民
- **Los Angeles** ロサンゼルス《米国の都市》
- **loss** 名 ①損失（額・物）, 損害, 浪費 ②失敗, 敗北
- **lot** 名 一区画, 用地
- **Louis Dynasty** ルイ王朝
- **Louisiana** ルイジアナ州
- **lover** 名 ①愛人, 恋人 ②愛好者
- **low-income** 形 低所得の
- **lower Manhattan** ロアー・マンハッタン《マンハッタン南部地域で,

America FAQ

ニューヨーク市の中心街》
- **loyalty** 名 忠義, 忠誠
- **lumber** 名 ①材木, 用材 ②がらくた
- **lyric** 名 歌詞, 叙事詩 形 歌の, 叙情的な

M

- **machine gun** 機関銃
- **machinery** 名 機械類［装置］
- **Macy's** 名 メーシーズ《米国の百貨店チェーン》
- **made** 熟 have something made ～を作らせる
- **mafia** 名 マフィア
- **magnitude** 名 マグニチュード《単位》
- **mailman** 名 郵便配達人
- **mailperson** 名 郵便配達人
- **main** 形 主な, 主要な
- **Maine** 名 メイン州
- **mainland** 名 本土, 大陸
- **mainly** 副 主に
- **mainstay** 名 頼みの綱, 大黒柱
- **mainstream** 名 主流, 本流, 大勢 形 主流の
- **maintain** 動 ①維持する ②養う
- **major** 形 大きいほうの, 主な, 一流の
- **majority** 名 ①大多数, 大部分 ②過半数
- **make** 熟 make a living 生計［暮らし］を立てる make ～ out of … ～を…から作る make friends with ～と友達になる make into ～を…に仕立てる make the rounds of ～を回って歩く make up 作り出す, 考え出す, ～を構成する
- **make-up** 名 ①化粧（品）, メーク, メーキャップ ②組み立て, 構造 ③性質, 体質
- **male** 形 男の, 雄の 名 男, 雄
- **mall** 名 モール, 広場
- **man-made** 形 人間が作り出した, 人工の
- **manage** 動 ①動かす, うまく処理する ②経営［管理］する, 支配する ③どうにか～する
- **management** 名 ①経営, 取り扱い ②運営, 管理（側）
- **mandate** 名 命令
- **Manhattan** 名 マンハッタン《地名》 lower Manhattan ロアー・マンハッタン《マンハッタン南部地域で, ニューヨーク市の中心街》
- **manned** 形 有人の
- **manufacture** 動 製造［製作］する 名 製造, 製作, 製品
- **manufacturer** 名 製造業者, メーカー
- **manufacturing** 名 製造（業）
- **many** 熟 as many as ～もの数の
- **Mariana Islands** マリアナ諸島
- **Marianas** 名 マリアナ諸島
- **marine corps** アメリカ海兵隊
- **mark** 名 （量や距離などの）到達点
- **marketing** 名 マーケティング
- **marriage** 名 結婚（生活・式）
- **married** 形 結婚した, 既婚の
- **marry** 動 結婚する
- **Mars** 名 火星
- **Marshall Islands** マーシャル諸島共和国
- **Martin Luther King, Jr. Day** マーティン・ルーサー・キング, ジュニア・デー《アメリカの祝日, 1月第3月曜日》
- **mascot** 名 マスコット
- **mass** 名 ①固まり,（密集した）集まり ②多数, 多量 ③《the -es》大衆 動 一団にする, 集める, 固まる

190

WORD LIST

- **Massachusetts** 名マサチューセッツ州
- **massacre** 名大虐殺, 皆殺し
- **master** 動〜の主となる
- **master's degree** 修士号
- **mastermind** 名黒幕, 首謀者
- **masterpiece** 名傑作, 名作, 代表作
- **material** 形①物質の, 肉体的な ②不可欠な, 重要な 名材料, 原料
- **materialistic** 形唯物論の, 物質主義の
- **matter** 熟 a matter of 〜の問題 as a matter of fact 実際は, 実のところ
- **Mayflower** 名メイフラワー号
- **mayor** 名市長, 町長
- **McKinley** 名《Mt.–》マッキンリー山
- **meaning** 名①意味, 趣旨 ②重要性
- **means** 名①手段, 方法 ②資力, 財産 ③mean (中間) の複数 means of 〜する手段
- **measure** 動①測る, (〜の) 寸法がある ②評価する 名①寸法, 測定, 計量, 単位 ②程度, 基準 take measures 手段を講じる
- **meddlesome** 形おせっかいな
- **media** 名メディア, マスコミ, 媒体
- **Medicaid** 名メディケイド《低所得者向け医療費補助制度》
- **medical** 形①医学の ②内科の 名健康診断, 身体検査
- **Medicare** 名メディケア《高齢者向け医療保険制度》
- **meeting** 名①集まり, ミーティング, 面会 ②競技会
- **melody** 名メロディー, 旋律
- **melt** 動①溶ける, 溶かす ②(感情が) 和らぐ, 次第に消え去る
- **melting pot** (人種・文化などの) るつぼ
- **memorial** 名記念物, 記録 形記念の, 追悼の
- **memorial day** 記念日
- **Memorial Day** 戦没者追悼記念日, メモリアル・デー《アメリカの公休日》
- **memory** 名①記憶(力), 思い出 ②(コンピュータの) メモリ, 記憶装置 in memory of 〜の記念として
- **mental** 形①心の, 精神の ②知能[知性] の
- **mentality** 名精神構造, メンタリティ, 考え方
- **merchant** 名商人, 貿易商
- **merge** 動合併する[させる], 融合する[させる], 溶け込む[ませる]
- **merging** 名結合, 融合
- **metal** 名金属, 合金
- **meteorologist** 名気象学者
- **method** 名①方法, 手段 ②秩序, 体系
- **Mexican** 形メキシコ(人) の 名メキシコ人
- **Mexican War** メキシコ戦争(メキシコ・アメリカ戦争)《1846-48》
- **Mexico** 名メキシコ《国名》 Gulf of Mexico メキシコ湾
- **Michigan** 名ミシガン湖
- **Mickey Mouse** ミッキーマウス
- **Microsoft Corporation** マイクロソフト《社名》
- **mid** 形中央の, 中間の
- **Mid-West** 名ミッドウェスト地域, アメリカ中西部
- **middle** 名中間, 最中 形中間の, 中央の
- **Middle East** 中東
- **Mideast** 名中東
- **midst** 名真ん中, 中央
- **Midwest** 名ミッドウェスト地域,

AMERICA FAQ

アメリカ中西部

- **Midwestern** 形アメリカ中西部の
- **might** 助《mayの過去》①～かもしれない ②～してもよい、～できる
- **mighty** 形強力な、権勢のある
- **mild** 形柔和な、温和な、口あたりのよい、穏やかな
- **military** 形軍隊[軍人]の、軍事の **Guantanamo military base** グァンタナモ米軍基地《キューバ東南部のグァンタナモ湾に位置するアメリカ海軍の基地》名《the –》軍、軍部
- **militia** 名市民軍、民兵
- **mind** 名①心、精神、考え ②知性 **bear in mind that** 心に留める
- **miner** 名炭鉱労働者、坑夫
- **Minnesota** 名ミネソタ州
- **minority** 名少数派、少数民族
- **minting** 名鋳造
- **mire** 動窮地[苦境]に陥る
- **mission** 名①使命、任務 ②使節団、代表団、派遣団 ③伝道、布教
- **missionary** 名宣教師、使節
- **Mississippi** 名ミシシッピ州
- **Mississippi River** ミシシッピ川
- **Missouri** 名ミズーリ州
- **mistaken** 形誤った
- **mixed** 形①混合の、混ざった ②男女共学の
- **mocking** 名あざ笑い
- **moderate** 動穏やかにする、抑える
- **modern** 形現代[近代]の、現代的な、最近の
- **Monroe** 名 (ジェームズ・)モンロー《第5代アメリカ合衆国大統領、任期1758–1825》
- **Monroe Doctrine** モンロー主義《欧州諸国による米大陸への干渉を拒否する宣言》
- **monster** 名怪物
- **Montana** 名モンタナ州
- **more** 熟 **ever more** これまで以上に
- **moreover** 副その上、さらに
- **Mormon** 名モルモン教徒
- **Mormon Church** モルモン教会
- **mortality** 名①死ぬ運命 ②死亡率、死亡者数
- **mosaic** 名モザイク、寄せ集め
- **most** 熟 **at most** せいぜい、多くても
- **mostly** 副主として、多くは、ほとんど
- **motion** 名①運動、移動 ②身振り、動作 ③(機械の)運転
- **move along** ～に沿って動く
- **moved** 形《be –》感激する、感銘する
- **movement** 名①動き、運動 ②《-s》行動 ③引っ越し ④変動 **civil rights movement** 公民権運動 **New Age movement** ニューエイジ運動 (1960年代後半から70年代にかけて流行した世界的なムーブメント)
- **moving** 形①動いている ②感動させる
- **Mt. McKinley** マッキンリー山
- **Mt. Whitney** ホイットニー山
- **much** 熟 **as much as** ～と同じだけ
- **muffler** 名①マフラー、えり巻き ②消音器
- **mulatto** 名ムラート(白人と黒人の)混血
- **multiply** 動①掛け算をする ②数が増える、繁殖する
- **murder** 名人殺し、殺害、殺人事件 動殺す
- **murderer** 名殺人犯

Word List

- **Murrah federal government building** オクラホマシティ連邦地方庁舎「アルフレッド・P・マラー」ビルディング
- **museum** 名 博物館, 美術館
- **musical** 形 音楽の 名 ミュージカル
- **musician** 名 音楽家
- **Muslim** 名 イスラム教徒, ムスリム 形 イスラム教［文明］の
- **mutiny** 名 船員や兵士の反抗, 反乱
- **mysterious** 形 神秘的な, 謎めいた

N

- **name after** ～にちなんで名付ける
- **naming** 名 ネーミング, 命名
- **Napoleon** 名 ナポレオン（・ボナパルト）《革命期フランスの軍人・政治家, フランス皇帝, 1769–1821》
- **Napoleonic Wars** ナポレオン戦争《1799年から1815年まで続いた, ナポレオン率いるフランスとイギリスの抗争を軸にした諸戦争の総称》
- **narrative-type** 形 語り口調の
- **NASA** 名 航空宇宙局
- **nation** 名 国, 国家,《the –》国民 **League of Nations** 国際連盟
- **national** 形 国家［国民］の, 全国の **national anthem** 国歌 **national holiday** 国民の休日 **national park** 国立公園
- **nationalism** 名 ナショナリズム, 国家主義
- **nationally** 副 全国的に
- **nationwide** 形 全国的な 副 全国的に, 全国では
- **native** 形 ①出生（地）の, 自国の ②(～に) 固有の, 生まれつきの, 天然の 名 (ある土地に) 生まれた人
- **Native American** 名 先住アメリカ人
- **naturalized** 形 帰化した
- **naturally** 副 生まれつき, 自然に, 当然
- **navy** 名 海軍, 海軍力
- **nearly** 副 ①近くに, 親しく ②ほとんど, あやうく
- **Nebraska** 名 ネブラスカ州
- **necessarily** 副 ①必ず, 必然的に, やむを得ず ②《not –》必ずしも～でない
- **necessary** 形 必要な, 必然の 名《-s》必需品, 必需品
- **necessity** 名 必要, 不可欠, 必要品
- **needle** 名 針, 針状のもの
- **negative** 形 否定的な, 消極的な
- **negotiation** 名 交渉, 話し合い
- **Negro** 名 黒人《歴史的文脈以外では蔑称》
- **neighborhood** 名 近所（の人々）, 付近
- **neighboring** 形 隣の, 近所の
- **neither** 副《否定文に続いて》～も…しない **neither ～ nor …** ～も…もない
- **Neoconservatism** 名 新保守主義
- **neon light** ネオンの光［サイン］
- **network** 名 回路, 網状組織, ネットワーク
- **neutrality** 名 中立（の状態・態度）
- **Nevada** 名 ネバダ州
- **nevertheless** 副 それにもかかわらず, それでもやはり
- **New Age movement** ニューエイジ運動《1960年代後半から70年代にかけて流行した世界的なムーブメント》
- **New Amsterdam** ニューアムステルダム《地名》

193

America FAQ

- **New Continent** 新大陸
- **New England** ニューイングランド地方《地名》
- **New Hampshire** ニューハンプシャー州
- **New Jersey** ニュージャージー州
- **New Mexico** ニューメキシコ州
- **New Orleans** ニューオーリンズ《都市名》
- **New World** アメリカ大陸, 新世界
- **New Year's Day** 元日
- **New York** ニューヨーク《米国の都市;州》
- **New York City** ニューヨーク市
- **New York Federal Reserve Bank** ニューヨーク連邦準備銀行
- **New York Philharmonic Orchestra** ニューヨーク・フィル(ハーモニック)交響楽団
- **New Yorker** ニューヨーク人, ニューヨーク居住者
- **newspaper** 名 新聞(紙)
- **nickel** 名 5セント《米国通貨》
- **nickname** 名 愛称, あだ名 動 あだ名をつける, 愛称で呼ぶ
- **Nile** 名 ナイル川
- **nineteenth** 名《通例the－》第19番目(の人[物]), 19日 形《通例the－》第19番目の
- **no doubt** きっと, たぶん
- **no longer** もはや〜でない[〜しない]
- **no one** 代 誰も[一人も]〜ない
  no one else 他の誰一人として〜しない
- **noise** 名 騒音, 騒ぎ, 物音
- **nominate** 動 ①指名する, 推薦する ②指定する
- **non-commercial** 形 非営利的な
- **non-contractual** 形 契約によらない, 非契約の
- **non-white** 形 非白人の
- **nonetheless** 副 それでもなお, それにもかかわらず
- **nor** 接 〜もまたない
- **norm** 名 基準, 規範
- **normal** 形 普通の, 平均の, 標準的な 名 平常, 標準, 典型
- **North America** 北アメリカ, 北米
- **North American** 北米の
- **North Carolina** ノースカロライナ州
- **North Korean** 北朝鮮の
- **northeast** 名 北東, 北東部
- **northern** 形 北の, 北向きの, 北からの
- **not 〜 but …** 〜ではなくて…
- **not only 〜 but (also) …** 〜だけでなく…もまた
- **notable** 形 注目に値する, 著名な, 重要な
- **note** 名 ①メモ, 覚え書き ②手形 bank note 紙幣 Federal Reserve note 連邦準備券 動 ①書き留める ②注意[注目]する
- **noticeable** 形 人目を引く, 目立つ, 著しい
- **not...not yet** まだ〜してない
- **notwithstanding** 前 〜にもかかわらず 副 それにもかかわらず
- **novelist** 名 小説家
- **nowadays** 副 このごろは, 現在では
- **nuance** 名 (表現などの)微妙な差異, ニュアンス
- **nude** 形 衣類をつけていない, 裸の 名 裸体(画)
- **number** 熟 a great number of 非常に多くの a number of いくつかの〜, 多くの〜

Word List

- **numerous** 形 多数の
- **nurture** 動 養育する, 育てる

O

- **Oakland Clippers** オークランド・クリッパーズ《サッカーチーム》
- **oath** 名 宣誓, 誓い
- **Obama** 名 (バラク・)オバマ《アメリカ合衆国の政治家。第44代大統領, 在任1961–》
- **obesity** 名 (病的な)肥満
- **object** 名 ①物, 事物 ②目的物, 対象
- **objection** 名 反対, 異議, 不服
- **oblige** 動 ①(〜を)余儀なくさせる, しいる ②要望にこたえる ③恩恵を与える, 《受け身形で》感謝している
- **observation** 名 観察(力), 注目
- **observe** 動 ①観察[観測]する, 監視[注視]する ②気づく ③守る, 遵守する
- **obtain** 動 ①得る, 獲得する ②一般に通用している
- **obvious** 形 明らかな, 明白な
- **obviously** 副 明らかに, はっきりと
- **occasion** 名 ①場合, (特定の)時 ②機会, 好機 ③理由, 根拠
- **occupation** 名 ①職業, 仕事, 就業 ②占有, 居住, 占領
- **occur** 動 (事が)起こる, 生じる, (考えなどが)浮かぶ
- **occurrence** 名 発生, 出来事
- **off-year election** 中間選挙
- **offer** 動 申し出る, 申し込む, 提供する
- **officer** 名 役人, 公務員, 警察官
- **officially** 副 公式に, 職務上, 正式に
- **offspring** 名 ①子孫, 子ども ②成果
- **Ohio** 名 オハイオ州
- **oil** 名 油, 石油
- **Oklahoma** 名 オクラホマ州
- **Oklahoma City** オクラホマシティー《都市名》
- **Old Black Joe** オールド・ブラック・ジョー《フォスター(Stephen Foster)が作詞作曲したアメリカ民謡》
- **Old Testament** 旧約聖書
- **on the outskirts of** 〜のはずれに
- **on-line shopping** オンライン・ショッピング
- **oneself** 代 自分自身
- **ongoing** 形 行われている, 進行している
- **Ontario** 名 オンタリオ湖
- **opening** 名 開始, 始め
- **openly** 副 率直に, 公然と
- **opera** 名 歌劇, オペラ
- **operation** 名 作戦, 軍事行動
- **opportunity** 名 好機, 適当な時期[状況]
- **oppose** 動 反対する, 敵対する
- **opposite** 形 反対の, 向こう側の
- **opposition** 名 反対
- **oppression** 名 圧迫, 抑圧, 重荷
- **oppressive** 形 圧制的な
- **optimism** 名 楽天主義, 楽観
- **orchestra** 名 管弦楽団, オーケストラ
- **order** 熟 in order to 〜するために, 〜しようと
- **Oregon** 名 オレゴン州
- **Oregon Trail** オレゴン・トレイル《19世紀, 北アメリカ大陸の西部開拓時代にアメリカ合衆国の開拓者達が通った主要道の一つ》

195

America FAQ

- **organic** 形 有機農法の, 化学肥料を用いない
- **organization** 名 団体, 機関
- **organize** 動 組織する
- **organized** 形 組織化された
- **Oriental** 形 東洋人の
- **oriented** 形 〜指向の, 〜を重視する
- **origin** 名 起源, 出自
- **original** 形 ①始めの, 元の, 本来の ②独創的な
- **originally** 副 ①元は, 元来 ②独創的に
- **originate** 動 始まる, 始める, 起こす, 生じる
- **Osama Bin Laden** オサマ・ビン・ラディン《サウジアラビア出身のイスラム過激派テロリスト。アルカイダの司令官、1957-2011》
- **other** 熟 on the other hand 一方, 他方では
- **out** 熟 keep out of 〜を避ける, 〜に干渉しない make 〜 out of … 〜を…から作る out of ①〜から外へ, 〜から抜け出して ②〜から作り出して, 〜を材料として ③〜の範囲外に, 〜から離れて ④(ある数)の中から
- **outbreak** 名 勃発, 発生
- **outnumber** 動 数で勝る, (〜より)多い
- **outright** 形 ①完全な ②明白な ③徹底した 副 完全に, 徹底的に
- **outsider** 名 よそ者, 部外者, 門外漢
- **outskirts** 熟 on the outskirts of 〜のはずれに
- **outstanding** 形 突出した, 際立った
- **over** 熟 all over 〜中で, 全体に亘って, 〜の至る所で, 全て終わって, もうだめで
- **over-application** 名 過剰適用
- **overall** 形 総体的な, 全面的な
- **overcome** 動 勝つ, 打ち勝つ, 克服する
- **overlook** 動 ①見落とす, (チャンスなどを)逃す ②見渡す ③大目に見る
- **overrun** 動 限度を超える, 超過する
- **overseas** 形 海外の, 外国の 副 海外へ 名 国外
- **overwhelm** 動 力で圧倒する, 苦しむ, 混乱する
- **overwhelming** 動 overwhelm (力で圧倒する)の現在分詞 形 圧倒的な, 圧勝の
- **own** 動 所有する 形 of one's own 自分自身の
- **owner** 名 持ち主, オーナー
- **oxcart** 名 牛車
- **oxen** 名 雄牛《oxの複数形》

P

- **Pacific** 形 太平洋(沿岸)の
- **Pacific Ocean** 太平洋
- **package** 名 包み, 小包, パッケージ
- **paid** 動 pay (払う)の過去, 過去分詞
- **painter** 名 画家, ペンキ屋
- **painting** 名 絵画, 油絵
- **pair** 名 (2つから成る)一対, 一組, ペア
- **Pakistan** 名 パキスタン《国名》
- **Palestinian** 名 パレスチナ人
- **palm** 名 手のひら(状のもの)
- **panic** 名 パニック, 恐慌
- **parent** 名 ①《-s》両親 ②先祖
- **Paris** 名 パリ《フランスの首都》
- **park** 名 national park 国立公園

Word List

- **parliament** 名 国会, 議会 **British Parliament** イギリス議会
- **part** 熟 **play a part** 役目を果たす **take part in** ～に参加する
- **part-timer** 名 パートタイマー, 非常勤で働く人
- **participate** 動 参加する, 加わる
- **particular** 形 ①特別の ②詳細な 名 事項, 細部,《-s》詳細 **in particular** 特に, とりわけ
- **particularly** 副 特に, とりわけ
- **partner** 名 配偶者, 仲間, 同僚
- **party** 名 **Democratic Party** 民主党 **Green Party** 緑の党
- **pass by** ～のそばを通る[通り過ぎる]
- **passage** 名 ①通過, 通行, 通路 ②一節, 経過
- **passenger** 名 乗客, 旅客
- **Passover** 名 過越の祭り《ユダヤ教》
- **passport** 名 パスポート,(通行)許可証
- **past** 形 過去の, この前の 名 過去(の出来事)
- **pasture** 名 牧場, 牧草(地)
- **patch** 名 継ぎはぎ, 継ぎ, 傷当て
- **patient** 名 病人, 患者
- **patriotic** 形 愛国的な
- **pattern** 名 ①柄, 型, 模様 ②手本, 模範
- **Pax Americana** パックス・アメリカーナ《米国の力による平和》
- **pay** 動 支払う, 払う, 報いる, 償う
- **PC** 略 パソコン
- **peacefully** 副 平和に, 穏やかに
- **peak** 名 頂点, 最高点
- **Pearl Harbor** パールハーバー, 真珠湾《地名》
- **peer** 名 同等の人, 同僚
- **pejorative** 形 軽蔑語, 悪口
- **penalty** 名 刑罰, 罰, ペナルティー
- **pending** 形 未解決の, ペンディングの
- **penetrate** 動 ①貫く, 浸透する ②見抜く
- **peninsula** 名 半島 **Korean Peninsula** 朝鮮半島
- **penny** 名 ①ペニー, ペンス《英国の貨幣単位。1/100ポンド》②《否定文で》小銭, びた一文
- **Pentagon** 名 米国国防総省
- **per** 前 ～につき, ～ごとに
- **per se** 正確な意味において(は)
- **percentage** 名 パーセンテージ, 割合, 比率
- **perception** 名 認識, 知覚(力), 認知, 理解(力)
- **perform** 動 ①(任務などを)行う, 果たす, 実行する ②演じる, 演奏する
- **performance** 名 ①実行, 行為 ②成績, できばえ, 業績 ③演劇, 演奏, 見世物
- **perhaps** 副 たぶん, ことによると
- **period** 名 ①期, 期間, 時代 ②ピリオド, 終わり
- **permanent** 形 永続する, 永久の, 長持ちする
- **permeate** 動 ～に浸透する
- **permission** 名 許可, 免許
- **permit** 動 ①許可する ②(物・事が)可能にする
- **perpetual** 形 永久の, 絶え間ない
- **Perry** 名 ペリー提督《アメリカ海軍の軍人, 日本の江戸時代に艦隊を率いて鎖国をしていた日本へ来航し, 開国させたことで知られる, 1794–1858》
- **persecute** 動 迫害する, 虐待する
- **persecution** 名 迫害, 虐待
- **persist** 動 ①固執する, 主張する ②続く, 存続する
- **personal** 形 ①個人の, 私的な ②

197

America FAQ

本人自らの
- **perspective** 名 ①遠近法 ②観点 ③見通し
- **persuade** 動 説得する, 促して〜させる
- **Pete Wilson** ピート・ウィルソン《アメリカの政治家, 1933−》
- **petroleum** 名 石油
- **pharmacist** 名 薬剤師
- **phase** 名 ①段階, 局面 ②側面, 様相
- **phenomenon** 名 ①現象, 事象 ②並はずれたもの[人]
- **Philharmonic Orchestra** 交響楽団 New York Philharmonic Orchestra ニューヨーク・フィル(ハーモニック)交響楽団
- **photo** 名 写真
- **phrase** 名 句, 慣用句, 名言
- **physical** 形 ①物質の, 物理学の, 自然科学の ②身体の, 肉体の
- **physically** 副 ①自然法則上, 物理的に ②肉体的に, 身体的に
- **pickup truck** (後部荷台が無蓋の)小型トラック
- **Pilgrims** 名 ピルグリム(・ファーザーズ)《1620年, メイフラワー号で北アメリカに移住したイギリス人入植者》
- **pin-up** 名 ピンナップ《通例女性のヌード写真》
- **pine** 名 マツ(松), マツ材
- **pioneer** 名 開拓者, 先駆者
- **pioneering** 形 草分け的な
- **pious** 形 敬虔な, 信仰深い
- **Pittsburgh Steelers** ピッツバーグ・スティーラーズ《アメリカンフットボールのチーム》
- **PKO** 略 平和維持活動
- **place** 熟 take place 行われる, 起こる
- **plain** 名 高原, 草原

- **planning** 名 立案, 開発計画
- **plantation** 名 大農園, 植林地
- **plate** 名 (プレート・テクトニクス理論の)プレート
- **play a part** 役目を果たす
- **player** 名 ①競技者, 選手, 演奏者, 俳優 ②演奏装置
- **plead** 動 ①嘆願する, 訴える ②弁護する, 弁解する
- **pleasant** 形 ①(物事が)楽しい, 心地よい ②快活な, 愛想のよい
- **pledge** 動 誓約する[させる], 誓う, 保障する
- **ply** 動 (定期的に)往復する
- **Plymouth** 名 プリマス《地名》
- **point** 熟 point of view 考え方, 視点 point out 指し示す, 指摘する, 目を向ける, 目を向けさせる turning point 転回点, 変わり目, ターニング・ポイント
- **polarized** 形 偏向した, 分極した
- **policeman** 名 警察官
- **policy** 名 ①政策, 方針, 手段 ②保険証券
- **policymaking** 名 政策決定, 政策立案
- **Polish** 形 ポーランド人の
- **political** 形 ①政治の, 政党の ②策略的な
- **politics** 名 政治(学), 政策
- **pollution** 名 汚染, 公害
- **polygamy** 名 複婚(制)
- **Pop art** ポップ・アート《1950年代後半にイギリスで生まれ, 1970年代まで続いた, 広告やコミックなどの大衆文化を取り入れた芸術運動》
- **popular among** 《be −》〜の間で人気がある
- **popularity** 名 人気, 流行
- **popularly** 副 一般に
- **population** 名 人口, 住民(数)

- **Porgy and Bess** 『ポーギーとベス』《オペラ, ジョージ・ガーシュウィン作曲, 1935》
- **port** 名 ①港, 港町, 空港 ②ポートワイン
- **Portland** 名 ポートランド《都市名》
- **portrait** 名 肖像画
- **pose** 動 ①ポーズをとる[とらせる] ②気取る, 見せかける ③引き起こす
- **position** 名 ①位置, 場所, 姿勢 ②立場, 状況
- **positive** 形 ①肯定的な ②明確な, 明白な, 確信している
- **possess** 動 ①持つ, 所有する ②(心などを)保つ, 制御する
- **possibility** 名 可能性, 見込み, 将来性
- **possible** 形 ①可能な ②ありうる, 起こりうる
- **post-Vietnam War** ベトナム戦争後
- **post-war era** 戦後
- **post-world-war** 世界大戦後
- **pot** 名 壺, (深い)なべ melting pot (人種・文化などの)るつぼ
- **Potomac river** ポトマック川
- **pour** 動 ①注ぐ, 浴びせる ②流れ出る, 流れ込む ③ざあざあ降る
- **poverty** 名 貧乏, 貧困, 欠乏, 不足
- **powerful** 形 力強い, 実力のある, 影響力のある
- **practical** 形 ①実際的な, 実用的な, 役に立つ ②経験を積んだ
- **practicality** 名 実用主義, 実際的であること
- **practically** 副 ①事実上, 実質的に ②ほとんど
- **prairie** 名 大草原, プレーリー
- **prairie schooner** プレーリースクーナー《大草原の帆船, 幌牛車の一種》
- **pray for** ～のために祈る
- **preach** 動 説教する, 説く
- **precision** 名 正確さ, 精密さ
- **precursor** 名 先駆者
- **predict** 動 予測[予想]する
- **predominantly** 副 大部分は, 圧倒的に
- **prefecture** 名 県, 府
- **preferential** 形 ①優遇の ②優先の, 優先的な
- **prejudice** 名 偏見, 先入観
- **premise** 名 ①前提 ②根拠 ③土地, 家屋
- **premium** 名 ①保険料, 保険の掛け金 ②奨励金 ③割り増し(料金)
- **preoccupation** 名 心を奪われること, 没頭
- **prepare for** 熟 ～の準備をする
- **prepared** 形 準備[用意]のできた
- **presence** 名 ①存在すること ②出席, 態度
- **present** 熟 at present 今のところ, 現在は, 目下
- **present-day** 形 今日の, 現代の
- **preservation** 名 保護, 保守
- **presidency** 名 大統領職
- **president** 名 ①大統領 ②社長, 学長, 頭取
- **presidential** 形 大統領の
- **pressure** 名 押すこと, 圧力, 重荷
- **prevail** 動 ①普及する ②勝つ, 圧倒する
- **prevent** 動 ①妨げる, じゃまする ②予防する, 守る, 《～ from …》～が…できない[しない]ようにする
- **previous** 形 前の, 先の
- **previously** 副 あらかじめ, 以前に[は]
- **price** 名 ①値段, 代価 ②《-s》物価, 相場
- **pride** 名 誇り, 自慢, 自尊心

199

America FAQ

- **primary** 形第一の, 主要な, 最初の, 初期の 名①第一のこと ②予備選挙
- **Prime Minister** 首相
- **principle** 名①原理, 原則 ②道義, 正道
- **printing** 名印刷
- **priority** 名優先(すること), 優先度[順位]
- **prison** 名①刑務所, 監獄 ②監禁
- **prisoner** 名囚人, 捕虜
- **private** 形①私的な, 個人の ②民間の, 私立の ③内密の, 人里離れた
- **pro league** プロリーグ
- **Pro Sports** プロスポーツ
- **pro-** 頭〜賛成の, 〜支持の
- **pro-abortionist** 名中絶賛成派
- **pro-British** 形親英の
- **pro-environmental** 形環境に配慮した
- **pro-football** 名プロフットボール
- **probably** 副たぶん, あるいは
- **probe** 動徹底的に調査する, 探りを入れる
- **procedure** 名手順, 手続き
- **proceed** 動進む, 進展する, 続ける
- **process** 名①過程, 経過, 進行 ②手順, 方法, 製法, 加工
- **Procter & Gamble** プロクター・アンド・ギャンブル《社名》
- **producer** 名プロデューサー, 製作者, 生産者
- **product** 名①製品, 産物 ②成果, 結果
- **production** 名製造, 生産
- **profession** 名職業, 専門職
- **professional** 形専門の, プロの, 職業的な
- **professor** 名教授, 師匠 visiting music professor 客員音楽教授
- **progress** 名①進歩, 前進 ②成り行き, 経過 動前進する, 上達する
- **prohibit** 動①禁止する, 差し止める ②妨げる, 予防する
- **prohibition** 名禁止, 差し止め
- **project** 名計画, プロジェクト
- **proliferation** 名拡散, 急増
- **prolific** 形繁殖力のある, 多産の
- **prominent** 形①突き出た ②傑出した, 目立つ
- **promised land** 約束の国, 天国
- **promising** 形有望な, 見込みのある
- **promote** 動促進する, 昇進[昇級]させる
- **promotion** 名①昇進 ②促進 ③宣伝販売
- **promotional** 形販促用の
- **promulgate** 動宣伝する, 広める, 推奨する
- **promulgation** 名発布, 普及
- **property** 名①財産, 所有物[地] ②性質, 属性
- **proportion** 名①割合, 比率, 分け前 ②釣り合い, 比例
- **propose** 動①申し込む, 提案する ②結婚を申し込む
- **prosecute** 動起訴する, 告訴する, 遂行する
- **prosecution** 名①遂行 ②起訴, 求刑 ③起訴側
- **prosecutor** 名①検察官 ②訴追者
- **prosper** 動栄える, 繁栄する, 成功する
- **prosperity** 名繁栄, 繁盛, 成功
- **prostitution** 名売春
- **protection** 名保護, 保護するもの[人]
- **protest** 名抗議(書), 不服
- **Protestant** 名プロテスタント

WORD LIST

White Anglo-Saxon Protestant ワスプ《アングルサクソン系白人プロテスタントおよびそれによって構成される階層》形 プロテスタントの
- **Protestantism** 名 プロテスタント主義
- **prove** 動 ①証明する ②(〜である ことが)わかる, (〜と)なる
- **provide** 動 ①供給する, 用意する, (〜に)備える ②規定する
- **provincial** 形 州の, 地方の, 県の
- **provision** 名 ①用意, 対策 ②食糧 ③規定, 条項
- **psychological** 形 心理学の, 精神の, 心理的な
- **public** 名 一般の人々, 大衆 形 公の, 公開の
- **publicize** 動 公表する, 広告する
- **Puerto Rico** プエルトリコ
- **pull out** 引き抜く, 引き出す, 取り出す
- **pumpkin** 名 ①カボチャ ②重要人物
- **pumpkin pie** パンプキン・パイ
- **punish** 動 罰する, ひどい目にあわせる
- **punishment** 名 ①罰, 処罰 ②罰を受けること capital punishment 極刑, 死刑
- **purchase** 動 購入する, 獲得する 名 購入(物), 仕入れ, 獲得
- **pursue** 動 ①追う, つきまとう ②追求する, 従事する
- **pursuit** 名 追跡, 追求
- **put 〜 into ...** 〜を…の状態にする, 〜を…に突っ込む
- **put aside** わきに置く
- **put up a fight** 抵抗する, 戦う

Q
- **quake** 動 ①ふるえる, おののく ②揺れる, 振動する
- **quality** 名 ①質, 性質, 品質 ②特性 ③良質
- **quarter** 名 25セント 動 4等分する
- **question** 熟 come into question 問題になる, 議論される
- **quickly** 副 敏速に, 急いで
- **quorum** (議決に必要な)定足数

R
- **race-related** 形 人種に関連した
- **racial** 形 人種の, 民族の
- **radical** 形 急進的な, 過激な
- **rage** 名 激怒, 猛威, 熱狂
- **railway** 名 鉄道
- **raise** 動 ①上げる, 高める ②起こす ③〜を育てる ④(資金を)調達する
- **rallying point** (さまざまな考え方などの)結集点
- **Ralph Nader** ラルフ・ネーダー《アメリカの弁護士・社会運動家, 1934-》
- **rampant** 形 (恐ろしいほどに)まん延した
- **range** 名 山脈
- **rank** 動 ①並ぶ, 並べる ②分類する
- **rap music** ラップ音楽
- **rape** 名 強姦, レイプ
- **rapidly** 副 速く, 急速, すばやく, 迅速に
- **rapper** 名 ラップミュージシャン
- **rate** 名 ①割合, 率 ②相場, 料金
- **rather** 副 ①むしろ, かえって ②かなり, いくぶん, やや ③それどころか逆に

America FAQ

- **rating** 名 ①格付け, 評価, 採点 ②視聴率 ③支持率 ④等級 ⑤(英国軍の) 下士官, 水兵
- **re-elect** 動 〜を再選する
- **reach down** 手を下に伸ばす
- **react** 動 反応する, 対処する
- **Reagan** 名 (ロナルド・) レーガン《アメリカ合衆国の俳優, 政治家。第40代アメリカ合衆国大統領, 任期 1981-1989》
- **realistic** 形 現実的な, 現実主義の
- **reality** 名 現実, 実在, 真実(性) **out of touch with reality** 現実離れして
- **realize** 動 理解する, 実現する
- **rebel** 動 反抗する, 反逆する
- **rebuilt** 動 rebuild (再建する) の過去, 過去分詞
- **recall** 動 呼び戻し, リコール
- **recent** 形 近ごろの, 近代の
- **recently** 副 近ごろ, 最近
- **recession** 名 景気後退, 不況, 後退
- **recognize** 動 認める, 認識 [承認] する
- **reconsider** 動 考え直す, 再検討する
- **record** 名 ①記録, 登録, 履歴 ②(音楽などの) レコード 動 ①記録 [登録] する ②録音 [録画] する
- **recoup** 動 取り戻す
- **recover** 動 ①取り戻す, ばん回する ②回復する
- **recovery** 名 回復, 復旧, 立ち直り
- **recruit** 動 (人材を) 募集する, 勧誘する
- **recruiter** 名 求人担当者
- **recruitment** 名 採用, 補充, 募集, 新兵募集
- **rededication** 名 再奉納, 再献納
- **reduce** 動 ①減じる ②しいて〜させる, (〜の) 状態にする
- **reduction** 名 ①下げること, 減少, 値下げ, 割引 ②縮図 ③換算, 約分, 還元
- **refer** 動 ①《 – to 〜》〜に言及する, 〜と呼ぶ, 〜を指す ②〜を参照する, 〜に問い合わせる
- **reference** 名 言及, 参照, 照会 **reference to** 〜への言及
- **reflect** 動 映る, 反響する, 反射する
- **reflection** 名 ①反射, (鏡・水などに) 映った姿, 映像 ②熟考
- **reform** 名 改善, 改良
- **refrain** 動 差し控える, 自制する
- **refreshment** 名 ①気分をすっきりさせること ②軽い食事 [飲み物], お茶菓子
- **refuge** 名 避難, 保護, 避難所
- **refuse** 動 拒絶する, 断る
- **regard** 動 ①(〜を…と) 見なす ②尊敬する, 重きを置く ③関係がある 名 ①注意, 関心 ②尊敬, 好感 ③《-s》(手紙などで) よろしくというあいさつ
- **regarding** 動 regard (見なす) の現在分詞 前 〜に関しては, 〜について
- **regime** 名 政体, 政権
- **region** 名 ①地方, 地域 ②範囲
- **regional** 形 地方の, 局地的な
- **registration** 名 登録, 記載, 登記
- **regulation** 名 規則, 規定, 規制
- **rejection** 名 拒絶, 不採用
- **relate** 動 ①関連がある, かかわる, うまく折り合う ②物語る
- **related** 動 relate (関係がある) の過去, 過去分詞 形 ①関係のある, 関連した ②姻戚の
- **relation** 名 ①(利害) 関係, 間柄 ②親戚
- **relationship** 名 関係, 関連, 血縁

202

Word List

関係
- **relative** 形 関係のある, 相対的な 名 親戚, 同族
- **relatively** 副 比較的, 相対的に
- **release** 動 解き放す, 釈放する
- **relevant** 形 関連した, 該当する
- **religion** 名 宗教, ～教, 信条
- **religious** 形 ①宗教の ②信心深い
- **relocation camp** 強制収容所
- **remain** 動 ①残っている, 残る ②(～の)ままである[いる] 名 《-s》①残り(もの) ②遺跡
- **remarkable** 形 ①異常な, 例外的な ②注目に値する, すばらしい
- **remedy** 動 治療する, (状況を)改善する
- **reminder** 名 思い出させるもの
- **reminiscent** 形 思い出させる, しのばせる, 連想させる, 追憶の
- **remove** 動 ①取り去る, 除去する ②(衣類を)脱ぐ
- **renegotiate** 動 再交渉する
- **repeal** 名 (法律などの)取り消し, 撤廃 動 無効にする, 撤廃する
- **reportedly** 形 伝えられるところでは
- **represent** 動 ①表現する ②意味する ③代表する
- **representation** 名 表現, 代表, 代理
- **representative** 名 ①代表(者), 代理人 ②代議士 ③典型, 見本 House of Representatives 下院 形 ①代表の, 代理の ②典型的な
- **reproduce** 動 ①再生する, 再現する ②複写する, 模造する
- **Republic of China** 中華民国
- **Republican** 名 共和党員 Congressional Republican 共和党議員
- **Republican party** 共和党
- **request** 動 求める, 申し込む
- **require** 動 ①必要とする, 要する ②命じる, 請求する
- **research** 名 調査, 研究 動 調査する, 研究する
- **resentment** 名 怒り, 立腹, うらみ
- **reserve** 動 ①とっておく, 備えておく ②予約する ③留保する 名 ①蓄え, 備え ②準備[積立]金 ③遠慮 Federal Reserve Bank 連邦準備銀行 Federal Reserve note 連邦準備券
- **reserved** 動 reserve(とっておく)の過去, 過去分詞 形 ①予約済みの, 貸し切りの ②遠慮がちの, よそよそしい
- **reside** 動 ①住む, 永住する ②(権利・性質などが～に)ある
- **resident** 名 居住者, 在住者
- **resist** 動 抵抗[反抗・反撃]する, 耐える
- **resource** 名 ①資源, 財産 ②手段, 方策
- **respect** 名 ①尊敬, 尊重 ②注意, 考慮 動 尊敬[尊重]する
- **respectively** 副 それぞれに, めいめい
- **respond** 動 答える, 返答[応答]する
- **responsibility** 名 ①責任, 義務, 義理 ②負担, 責務
- **restoration** 名 ①回復, 復活, 修復 ②《the R-》王政復古
- **restore** 動 元に戻す, 復活させる
- **restrain** 動 ①(人・動物の行動を)制する, 抑制する ②こらえる ③拘束する
- **restrict** 動 制限する, 禁止する
- **restriction** 名 制限, 規制
- **result** 名 結果, 成り行き, 成績 as a result その結果(として) as a result of ～の結果(として) 動 (結

America FAQ

果として)起こる, 生じる, 結局〜になる
- **retail** 形小売りの 名小売り(店)
- **retailer** 名小売り業者, 小売り商売をする人, 小売り店
- **retirement** 名引退, 退職
- **retrofit** 形改良する, 変更する
- **Rev.** 略師, 牧師
- **revel** 動大いに楽しむ, 酒盛りをする
- **revenue** 名所得, 収入, 利益, (国の)歳入
- **reverberation** 名反射, 反響, 残響
- **reverse** 形反対の, 裏側の 動逆にする, 覆す
- **review** 名①書評, 評論 ②再調査 ③復習
- **revive** 動生き返る, 生き返らせる, 復活する[させる]
- **revoke** 動〜を取り消す, 破棄する
- **revolution** 名①革命, 変革 ②回転, 旋回
- **Revolutionary Army** 革命軍
- **revolutionize** 動大変革[革命]をもたらす, 根本的に変える
- **Rhode Island** ロードアイランド州
- **rhythm** 名リズム, 調子
- **Richter scale** リヒター・スケール《マグニチュード, 地震が発するエネルギーの大きさを表した指標値》
- **ridge** 名尾根, 棟
- **riding** 名乗馬
- **riot** 名暴動, 騒動
- **rioter** 名暴徒
- **ripple effect** 名波及効果, 連鎖反応
- **rise** 熟 give rise to 〜を引き起こす
- **risk** 名危険
- **risk-taking** 形危険[リスク]をいとわない
- **ritual** 名①儀式 ②行事 ③慣例
- **rival** 名競争相手, 匹敵する人 動競争する
- **roam** 動ぶらぶら歩き回る, 放浪する
- **roasted turkey** 七面鳥の丸焼き
- **Rock 'n' Roll** ロックンロール
- **Rockefeller Center** ロックフェラー・センター
- **rocket** 名ロケット heavy lift rocket 重量物打ち上げロケット
- **Rockies** 名ロッキー山脈
- **Rocky Mountains** ロッキー山脈
- **role** 名①(劇などの)役 ②役割, 任務 leading role 主導的役割
- **roll** 名①一巻き ②転がること, 転がすこと
- **rolled** 形巻いた
- **Ronald Reagan** ロナルド・レーガン《アメリカ合衆国の俳優, 政治家。第40代アメリカ合衆国大統領, 任期1981–1989》
- **Roosevelt** 名①(フランクリン・デラノ・)ルーズベルト《アメリカ合衆国の政治家, 第32代アメリカ大統領, 任期1933–1945》②(セオドア・)ルーズベルト《アメリカ合衆国の第25代副大統領および第26代大統領, 大統領任期, 1901–1901》
- **root** 名①根, 根元 ②根源, 原因 ③《-s》先祖, ルーツ take root 根づく, 定着する
- **Ross Perot** ロス・ペロー《アメリカ合衆国の実業家であり政治家, 1930–》
- **roughly** 副①おおよそ, 概略的に, 大ざっぱに ②手荒く, 粗雑に
- **round** 熟 make the rounds of 〜を回って歩く
- **row** 名 death row 死刑囚房房
- **Roy Lichtenstein** ロイ・リキテ

- ンスタイン《ポップ・アートの代表的な画家, 1923–1997》
- **rugby** 名 ラグビー
- **ruin** 名 破滅, 滅亡, 破産, 廃墟
- **run counter to** 〜に逆行する
- **run-down** 形 荒廃した
- **rush** 動 突進する, せき立てる **rush into** 〜に突入する, 〜に駆けつける, 〜に駆け込む 名 突進, 突撃, 殺到 **Gold Rush** ゴールドラッシュ《カリフォルニアのサクラメントの近くで1848年に金鉱が発見され, 世界中で一攫千金を夢見るおびただしい移民が殺到した, 1848–1855》
- **Russia** 名 ロシア《国名》
- **rustic** 形 田舎風の, 素朴な, 田舎くさい

S

- **sacred** 形 神聖な, 厳粛な
- **Saddam Hussein** サダム・フセイン《イラク共和国の政治家, 1937–2006》
- **sail** 名 ①帆, 帆船 ②帆走, 航海 **set sail** 出帆[出航]する 動 ①帆走する, 航海する ②滑らかに飛ぶ
- **saint** 名 聖人, 聖徒
- **Saipan** 名 サイパン島
- **sales** 形 販売の
- **Salt Lake City** ソルトレークシティー《都市名》
- **Sam Houston** サミュエル・ヒューストン《アメリカの軍人, 政治家。テキサス州ヒューストンの名の由来となった, 1793–1863》
- **San Andreas fault** サンアンドレアス断層
- **San Antonio** サンアントニオ《地名》
- **San Francisco** サンフランシスコ《都市名》
- **San Jose** サンノゼ《地名》
- **sanction** 名 ①制裁(措置) ②承認, 認可
- **sand** 名 ①砂 ②《-s》砂漠, 砂浜
- **satisfactory** 形 満足な, 十分な
- **Saudi Arabia** 名 サウジアラビア《国名》
- **savings** 名 貯蓄金
- **scale** 名 ①目盛り ②規模, 割合, 程度, スケール **Richter scale** リヒター・スケール《マグニチュード, 地震が発するエネルギーの大きさを表した指標値》
- **scandal** 名 スキャンダル, 醜聞
- **scar** 名 傷跡
- **scatter** 動 ①ばらまく, 分散する ②《be -ed》散在する
- **scenery** 名 風景, 景色
- **schooner** 名 スクーナー船《縦帆の帆船》 **prairie schooner** プレーリースクーナー《大草原の帆船, 幌牛車の一種》
- **science-is-everything** 形 科学万能の
- **scientific** 形 科学の, 科学的な
- **scientifically** 副 科学的に, 学術的に
- **scoop** 動 すくい上げる, かき集める
- **Scottish** 名 スコットランド人
- **scream** 名 金切り声, 絶叫
- **search** 動 捜し求める, 調べる 名 捜査, 探索, 調査
- **seasonal** 形 季節の
- **Seattle** 名 シアトル《都市》
- **seaweed** 名 海藻, 海草
- **secede** 動 脱退する, 離脱する
- **seclusion** 名 鎖国
- **secret** 名 秘密
- **secretly** 副 秘密に, 内緒で
- **sect** 名 派閥, 学派, 宗派

AMERICA FAQ

- **secure** 動①安全にする ②確保する, 手に入れる
- **security** 名①安全(性), 安心 ②担保, 抵当,《-ties》有価証券 **US-Japan Security Treaty** 日米安全保障条約
- **see ~ as ...** ~を…と考える
- **see if** ~かどうかを確かめる
- **seek** 動 捜し求める, 求める
- **seem** 動(~に)見える,(~のように)思われる **seem to be** ~であるように思われる
- **seemingly** 副 見たところでは, 外見は
- **seen as**《be –》~として見られる
- **segment** 名 部分, 区分
- **segregation** 名 分離, 隔離, 人種差別
- **select** 動 選択する, 選ぶ
- **self-assertion** 名 出しゃばり
- **self-confidence** 名 自信
- **self-protection** 名 自己防衛
- **senator** 名 上院議員, 元老院議員,(大学の)評議員
- **senior** 形 年長の, 年上の, 古参の, 上級の 名 年長者, 先輩, 先任者
- **sensation** 名①感覚, 感じ ②大評判, センセーション
- **sense** 名①感覚, 感じ ②《-s》意識, 正気, 本性 ③常識, 分別, センス ④意味 動 感じる, 気づく
- **sensibility** 名 感覚, 識別能力,《-ties》感受性
- **sensitive** 形 敏感な, 感度がいい, 繊細な
- **sentence** 名①文 ②判決, 宣告 **life sentence** 終身刑 動 判決を下す, 宣告する
- **separate** 動①分ける, 分かれる, 隔てる ②別れる, 別れさせる 形 分かれた, 別れた, 別々の
- **separation** 名 分離(点), 離脱, 分類, 別離
- **series** 名 一続き, 連続, シリーズ
- **serious** 形①まじめな, 真剣な ②重大な, 深刻な,(病気などが)重い
- **servant** 名①召使, 使用人, しもべ ②公務員,(公共事業の)従業員
- **service** 名①勤務, 業務 ②公益事業
- **set out** ①出発する, 置く ②配置する
- **set sail** 出帆[出航]する
- **set up** 配置する, セットする, 据え付ける
- **setting** 名 設定, 周囲の環境
- **settle** 動①安定する[させる], 落ち着く, 落ち着かせる ②《-in ~》~に移り住む, 定住する
- **settlement** 名①定住, 入植地, 集落 ②合意, 解決, 清算
- **settler** 名 移住者, 入植者
- **seventeenth** 名 17, 17人[個] 形 17の, 17人[個]の
- **Seventh Avenue**(マンハッタンの)7番街
- **severely** 副 厳しく, 簡素に
- **sex** 名 性, 性別, 男女
- **sex-related** 形 性関連の
- **sexual** 形 性の, 性的な, セクシャルな
- **sexuality** 名 性的興味, 性欲
- **sexually harasses** セクハラ[性的嫌がらせ]をする
- **shadow** 名①影, 暗がり ②亡霊 **cast a shadow**(暗い)影を落とす
- **shape** 名①形, 姿, 型 ②状態, 調子
- **sharp** 形①鋭い, とがった ②刺すような, きつい ③鋭敏な ④急な
- **sharply** 副 鋭く, 激しく, はっきりと
- **sheer** 形①まったくの, 純粋の ②

206

切り立った
- **shellfish** 名 貝, 甲殻類《カニ, エビなど》
- **shelve** 動 (棚に)のせる, 棚上げする
- **shift** 動 移す, 変える, 転嫁する 名 ①変化, 移動 ②交替, (交代制の)勤務(時間), シフト
- **shocking** 形 衝撃的な, ショッキングな
- **shoot up** 燃え上がる
- **shooting** 名 撮影
- **shooting gallery** 麻薬常用者のたまり場
- **shopping** 名 買い物
- **shopping mall** ショッピングモール, 商店街
- **shore** 名 岸, 海岸, 陸
- **shown** 動 show(見せる)の過去分詞
- **side** 名 側, 横, そば, 斜面 on either side 両側に
- **sideline** 名 第三者の立場
- **Sierra Nevada** シエラネバダ《地名》
- **sight** 熟 catch sight of ～を見つける, ～を見かける in sight 視野に入って
- **significant** 形 ①重要な, 有意義な ②大幅な, 著しい ③意味ありげな
- **Silicon Valley** シリコン・バレー
- **similar** 形 同じような, 類似した, 相似れ be similar to ～に似ている
- **similarly** 副 同様に, 類似して, 同じように
- **simple-minded** 形 うぶな, 愚かな, 頭の弱い
- **simplicity** 名 単純, 質素
- **simplified** 形 簡易化した
- **simply** 副 ①簡単に ②単に, ただ ③まったく, 完全に
- **single** 形 たった1つの
- **sinking** 名 沈没
- **situation** 名 ①場所, 位置 ②状況, 境遇, 立場
- **sixteenth** 名 第16番目(の人[物]), 16日 形 第16番目の
- **sky-high** 形 とてつもなく高い
- **Skype** スカイプ《無料IP通話サービス》
- **slang** 名 俗語, スラング
- **slave** 名 奴隷
- **slavery** 名 奴隷制度, 奴隷状態
- **slide** 名 滑ること, 滑走
- **slight** 形 ①わずかな ②ほっそりして ③とるに足らない
- **slightly** 副 わずかに, いささか
- **slogan** 名 スローガン, モットー
- **sloping** 形 傾斜した
- **slum** 名 《-s》スラム街 inner-city slum 都心のスラム街
- **smallpox** 名 天然痘
- **smog** 名 スモッグ
- **smoke** 名 煙, 煙状のもの
- **smuggle** 動 密輸する
- **snap** 動 ①ぽきっと折る, ぶつんと切る ②ぱたんと閉じる[閉まる]
- **Snow White** 白雪姫
- **so** 熟 and so そこで, それだから, それで and so forth など, その他 so ～ that … 非常に～なので… so to speak いわば
- **so-called** 形 いわゆる
- **soar** 動 高く飛ぶ, 舞い上がる, 急騰する, 高くそびえる
- **soaring** 形 空にそびえる
- **soccer** 名 サッカー
- **soccer-loving** 形 サッカー好きの
- **social** 形 ①社会の, 社会的な ②社交的な, 愛想のよい

America FAQ

- **social studies** 社会科
- **socially disadvantaged** 社会的弱者
- **society** 名社会, 世間
- **soft drink** ソフトドリンク, 清涼飲料
- **software** 名ソフト(ウェア)
- **soil** 名土, 土地
- **solar system** 太陽系
- **soldier** 名兵士, 兵卒
- **solely** 副1人で, 単独で, 単に
- **solution** 名①分解, 溶解 ②解決, 解明, 回答
- **solve** 動解く, 解決する
- **somebody** 代誰か, ある人
- **someone** 代ある人, 誰か
- **something** 代①ある物, 何か ②いくぶん, 多少
- **sometimes** 副時々, 時たま
- **somewhat** 副いくらか, やや, 多少
- **sophistication** 名①洗練 ②世間慣れ ③精巧化
- **sorely** 副ひどく
- **sort** 名種類, 品質 **a sort of** 〜のようなもの, 一種の〜
- **sought** 動seek (捜し求める)の過去, 過去分詞
- **soul** 名①魂 ②精神, 心
- **source** 名源, 原因, もと
- **South Carolina** サウスカロライナ州
- **South San Francisco** サウスサンフランシスコ《地名》
- **southeast** 名南東(部)
- **Southeast Asia** 東南アジア
- **Southeast Asian** 東南アジアの人
- **southern** 形南の, 南向きの, 南からの

- **Southern California** 南カリフォルニア
- **Southern Hospitality** 米国南部の温かいもてなし
- **Southern pride** 南部の誇り
- **southerner** 名南部人
- **southwest** 名南西(部)
- **sovereign** 形①君主である, 最高権力を持つ ②独立した
- **sovereignty** 名①主権, 統治権 ②独立国家
- **Soviet Union** ソビエト連邦
- **space-related** 形宇宙関連の
- **spaceship** 名宇宙船
- **Spain** 名スペイン《国名》
- **spangled** 形ぴかぴか光る
- **Spanish** 形スペイン(人・語)の 名①スペイン人 ②スペイン語
- **spark** 名①火花 ②ひらめき, 輝き
- **speak** 動 **so to speak** いわば **speak of** 〜を口にする
- **specific** 形明確な, はっきりした, 具体的な
- **specify** 動詳細に述べる, 指定する, 明確に述べる
- **spectator** 名観客, 見物人
- **speculator** 名①思索家, 投機家 ②相場師
- **spending** 名支出, 出費
- **sphere** 名①球体, 天体 ②範囲, 分野
- **spirit** 名①霊 ②精神, 気力
- **splendid** 形見事な, 壮麗な, 堂々とした
- **spot** 名地点, 場所
- **spread out** 広げる, 展開する
- **Springfield** 名スプリングフィールド《都市名》
- **spy** 名スパイ
- **square** 名広場 **Tiananmen**

Word List

- Square 天安門広場 Times Square タイムズ・スクウェア
- ☐ **squarely** 副 四角に, 公正に
- ☐ **St. Lawrence River** セント・ローレンス川
- ☐ **stability** 名 安定(性), 持続
- ☐ **stabilization** 名 安定化
- ☐ **stabilize** 動 安定する, 固定する
- ☐ **stable** 形 安定した, 堅固な, 分解しにくい
- ☐ **stage** 名 ①舞台 ②段階
- ☐ **staggering** 動 stagger(よろめく)の現在分詞 形 よろめく, ふらつく
- ☐ **stagnant** 形 よどんだ, 流れない
- ☐ **stagnation** 名 沈滞, 不振
- ☐ **stance** 名 心構え, 立場
- ☐ **standard** 名 標準, 規格, 規準 形 ①標準の ②一流の, 優秀な
- ☐ **standardize** 動 規格化する, 標準化する, 統一する
- ☐ **Star-Spangled Banner** 星条旗
- ☐ **starting point** 出発点
- ☐ **startling** 動 startle(びっくりさせる)の現在分詞 形 びっくりさせる, 仰天させる
- ☐ **state** 名 ①あり様, 状態 ②国家, (アメリカなどの)州 ③階層, 地位
- ☐ **statistic** 名 統計値, 統計量
- ☐ **statistics** 名 統計(学), 統計資料
- ☐ **statue** 名 像
- ☐ **status** 名 ①(社会的な)地位, 身分, 立場 ②状態
- ☐ **staunchly** 副 断固として
- ☐ **stay afloat** (商売などを)なんとか成り立たせる
- ☐ **steadily** 副 しっかりと
- ☐ **steady** 形 ①しっかりした, 安定した, 落ち着いた ②堅実な, まじめな
- ☐ **steamboat** 名 蒸気船
- ☐ **steel** 名 鋼, 鋼鉄(製の物)
- ☐ **steep** 形 険しい
- ☐ **stem** 名 茎, (木の)幹 stem from the fact that ~という事実から生じる
- ☐ **Stephen Foster** スティーブン・フォスター《アメリカ合衆国を代表する歌曲作曲家, 1826-1864》
- ☐ **steppe** 名 大草原地帯
- ☐ **stereotyped** 形 型にはまった
- ☐ **stick** 動 くっつく, くっつける
- ☐ **stimulate** 動 ①刺激する ②促す, 活性化させる ③元気づける
- ☐ **stimulus** 名 刺激(物), 激励
- ☐ **stipulate** 動 (契約条項として)規定する, 要求する, 保証する
- ☐ **stock** 名 株式
- ☐ **stock-market** 形 株式市場の
- ☐ **storm** 名 ①嵐, 暴風雨 ②強襲 take the world by storm 世界を席巻する
- ☐ **straddle** 動 またがる
- ☐ **straight** 熟 go straight on 一直線に進む
- ☐ **strata** 名 階層, 層《stratumの複数形》
- ☐ **strategic** 形 戦略的な, 戦略上の
- ☐ **strategy** 名 戦略, 作戦, 方針
- ☐ **strength** 名 ①力, 体力 ②長所, 強み ③強度, 濃度
- ☐ **strengthen** 動 強くする, しっかりさせる
- ☐ **strengthening** 名 強化
- ☐ **stress** 名 ①圧力 ②ストレス ③強勢 動 ①強調する ②圧力を加える
- ☐ **stretch** 動 引き伸ばす, 広がる, 広げる 名 ①伸ばす[伸びる]こと, 広がり ②ストレッチ(運動)
- ☐ **strict** 形 厳しい, 厳密な
- ☐ **strictly** 副 厳しく, 厳密に
- ☐ **striking** 形 著しい, 目立つ

America FAQ

- **stripe** 名筋, 縞, ストライプ
- **stronghold** 名拠点, 本拠地
- **strongly** 副強く, 頑丈に, 猛烈に, 熱心に
- **structure** 名構造, 骨組み, 仕組み 動組織立てる
- **struggle** 動もがく, 奮闘する 名もがき, 奮闘
- **strung** 動 string（糸をつける）の過去, 過去分詞
- **stubborn** 形頑固な, 強情な
- **studio** 名①スタジオ, 仕事場 ②ワンルームマンション
- **stumble** 動①よろめく, つまずく ②偶然出会う 名つまずき
- **stupidity** 名おろかさ, おろかな考え[行為]
- **sturdy** 形屈強な, 頑丈な
- **style** 名やり方, 流儀, 様式, スタイル
- **submarine** 名潜水艦 形海底の
- **subprime loan** サブプライムローン《信用度の低い顧客に高い金利で貸し出す融資》
- **subsequent** 形次の, 続いて起きる, その結果生じた
- **subsequently** 副その後, それに続いて
- **subsist on** ～で生きている, ～を常食とする
- **subtle** 形微妙な, かすかな, 繊細な, 敏感な, 器用な
- **subtropical** 形亜熱帯の
- **suburb** 名近郊, 郊外
- **subway** 名地下鉄, 地下道
- **succeed** 動①成功する ②（～の）跡を継ぐ
- **success** 名成功, 幸運, 上首尾
- **successful** 形成功した, うまくいった
- **succession** 名連続, 相続, 継承
- **such** 熟 as such ～など such ～ as …… …のような～ such as たとえば～, ～のような
- **sudden** 形突然の, 急な
- **suffer** 動①（苦痛・損害などを）受ける, こうむる ②（病気に）なる, 苦しむ, 悩む
- **suited** 形適した
- **Super Bowl** スーパーボウル《アメリカンフットボール最大のプロリーグ, NFLの優勝決定戦》
- **superior** 名優れた人, 目上（の人）
- **Superior** 名スペリオル湖
- **supermarket** 名スーパーマーケット
- **superpower** 名超大国, 強国, 異常な力
- **superstar** 名スーパースター, 大スター
- **supplementary** 形補足の, 補助的な
- **supply** 動供給[配給]する, 補充する
- **support** 動①支える, 支持する ②養う, 援助する 名①支え, 支持 ②援助, 扶養
- **suppression** 名鎮圧, 抑制, 隠蔽
- **Supreme Court** 最高裁判所
- **surpass** 動勝る, しのぐ
- **surplus** 名余り, 残り, 余分, 余剰, 黒字
- **surprising** 形驚くべき, 意外な
- **surprisingly** 副驚くほど（に）, 意外にも
- **surrender** 動降伏する, 引き渡す
- **surround** 動囲む, 包囲する
- **survival** 名生き残ること, 生存者, 残存物
- **survive** 動①生き残る, 存続する, なんとかなる ②長生きする, 切り抜ける
- **surviving** 形生き残った

Word List

- **suspended** 形 停止した
- **suspension** 名 (一時的な)停止, 延期
- **suspicion** 名 ①容疑, 疑い ②感づくこと
- **suspicious** 形 あやしい, 疑い深い
- **sustain** 動 持ちこたえる, 持続する, 維持する, 養う
- **sway** 名 揺れ, 動揺
- **sweat** 名 汗
- **sweep** 名 (土地の)広がり
- **swell** 動 ①ふくらむ, ふくらませる ②増加する, 増やす
- **switch** 動 ①スイッチを入れる[切る] ②切り替える, 切り替わる
- **symbol** 名 シンボル, 象徴
- **symbolic** 形 象徴する, 象徴的な
- **symbolically** 副 象徴的に
- **symbolize** 動 ①記号を用いる ②象徴する, 象徴とみなす
- **sympathetic** 形 同情する, 思いやりのある
- **synonymous** 形 同意語の, 同義の

T

- **taboo** 形 タブーの, 禁止された
- **tailor** 動 (服を)仕立てる, 注文で作る
- **Taiwan** 名 台湾
- **take** 熟 take care of ~の世話をする, ~面倒を見る, ~を管理する take heed of ~に留意する take into 手につかむ, 中に取り入れる take measures 手段を講じる take over 引き継ぐ, 支配する, 乗っ取る take part in ~に参加する take place 行われる, 起こる take root 根づく, 定着する take the world by storm 世界を席巻する take up 取り上げる, 拾い上げる, やり始める, (時間・場所を)とる
- **talent** 名 才能, 才能ある人
- **talented** 形 才能のある, 有能な
- **Taliban** 名 タリバン《アフガニスタンのイスラム原理主義組織》
- **tame** 動 飼いならす, 従わせる
- **target** 名 標的, 目的物, 対象
- **task** 名 (やるべき)仕事, 職務, 課題
- **taste** 名 ①味, 風味 ②好み, 趣味
- **tattoo** 名 入れ墨
- **Taurus** 名 トーラス《車名》
- **tavern** 名 居酒屋, 酒場
- **tax** 名 ①税 ②重荷, 重い負担
- **taxpayer** 名 納税者
- **technology** 名 テクノロジー, 科学技術
- **tectonic** 形 地質構造の, 地殻変動の[による]
- **teem with** ~で満ちあふれている
- **telecommunication** 名 遠隔通信, 電気通信
- **telecommunications** 名 電気通信
- **telecommute** 動 在宅勤務をする
- **temperament** 名 気質, 気性
- **temperature** 名 温度, 体温
- **Temple in Jerusalem** エルサレム神殿
- **tempo** 名 テンポ, 速さ
- **tend** 動 ①(~の)傾向がある, (~)しがちである ②向かう, 行く
- **tendency** 名 傾向, 風潮, 性癖
- **tension** 名 緊張(関係), ぴんと張ること
- **tent** 名 テント, 天幕
- **term** 名 ①期間, 期限 ②語, 用語 ③《-s》条件 ④《-s》関係, 仲 in

America FAQ

terms of ～の言葉で言えば，～の点から
- **territory** 名①領土 ②(広い)地域，範囲，領域
- **terror** 名①恐怖 ②恐ろしい人[物] War on Terror テロへの戦い
- **terrorism** 名テロ行為，暴力行為
- **terrorist** 名テロリスト
- **Texas** 名テキサス州
- **textbook** 名教科書
- **Thailand** 名タイ《国名》
- **Thanksgiving Day** 感謝祭《祝日，11月の第4木曜日》
- **theater** 名劇場
- **theft** 名盗み，窃盗，泥棒
- **theme** 名主題，テーマ，作文
- **then-fashionable** 形当時流行の
- **Theodore Roosevelt** セオドア・ルーズベルト《アメリカ合衆国の第25代副大統領および第26代大統領，大統領任期，1901-1901》
- **theory** 名理論，学説 Darwin's theory of evolution ダーウィンの進化論
- **thereafter** 副それ以来，従って
- **therefore** 副したがって，それゆえ，その結果
- **these days** このごろ
- **thick** 形厚い，密集した，濃厚な
- **think of** ～のことを考える，～を思いつく，考え出す
- **thinking** 名考えること，思考
- **third-party** 形第三者の
- **this way** このように
- **Thomas Edison** トーマス・エジソン《アメリカ合衆国の発明家，起業家，1847-1931》
- **Thomas Jefferson** トーマス・ジェファーソン《第3代アメリカ合衆国大統領，1801-1809》
- **those** 熟 in those days あのころは，当時は those who ～する人々
- **though** 接①～にもかかわらず，～だが ②たとえ～でも even though ～であるけれども，～にもかかわらず 副しかし
- **threat** 名おどし，脅迫
- **threaten** 動脅かす，おびやかす，脅迫する
- **thrilling** 形スリル満点の，ぞくぞくする
- **thriving** 形繁盛している，盛況な
- **throughout** 前①～中；～を通じて ②～のいたるところに 副初めから終わりまで，ずっと
- **thrust** 動①強く押す，押しつける，突き刺す ②張り出す，突き出る
- **thunderstorm** 名(激しい)雷雨
- **thus** 副①このように ②これだけ ③かくて，だから
- **Tiananmen Square** 天安門広場
- **time** 熟 all the time ずっと，いつも，その間ずっと at a time 一度に，続けざまに at one time ある時は，かつては at that time その時 at the time そのころ，当時は by the time ～する時までに from time to time ときどき in time 間に合って，やがて of the time 当時の，当節の times as … as A A の～倍の…
- **Times Square** タイムズ・スクウェア
- **title** 名①題名，タイトル ②肩書，称号 ③権利，資格
- **To Anacreon in Heaven** 「天国のアナクレオンへ」《アメリカ合衆国国歌「星条旗」になった曲。イギリスの作曲家，ジョン・スタフォード・スミス作》
- **ton** 名①トン《重量・容積単位》 ②《-s》たくさん
- **tongue** 名①舌 ②弁舌 ③言語
- **tonic** 名強壮剤，養毛剤，ヘアトニ

Word List

ック
- **tool** 名道具, 用具, 工具
- **top** 熟 on top of ～の上(部)に
- **tornado** 名竜巻, トルネード
- **Tornado Alley** 竜巻街道, 竜巻多発地帯
- **torrential** 形圧倒的な, 猛烈な, おびただしい
- **torture** 動拷問にかける, ひどく苦しめる
- **total** 形総計の, 全体の, 完全な 名全体, 合計 動合計する
- **totally** 副全体的に, すっかり
- **touch** 熟 out of touch with reality 現実離れして
- **tough** 形堅い, 丈夫な, たくましい, 骨の折れる, 困難な
- **tourist** 名旅行者, 観光客
- **trace** 動たどる, さかのぼって調べる
- **tracklayer** 名保線作業員
- **trade** 名取引, 貿易, 商業
- **trading** 名貿易, 通商
- **tradition** 名伝統, 伝説, しきたり
- **traditional** 形伝統的な
- **traditionalism** 名伝統主義
- **traditionally** 副伝統的に, 元々は
- **tragic** 形悲劇の, 痛ましい
- **trail** 名(通った)跡 Oregon Trail オレゴン・トレイル《19世紀, 北アメリカ大陸の西部開拓時代にアメリカ合衆国の開拓者達が通った主要道の一つ》動ひきずる, 跡を追う trail behind ～に遅れを取る
- **transaction** 名①取引 ②処理, 取り扱い
- **Transcontinental Railway** 大陸横断鉄道
- **transfer** 動①移動する ②移す ③譲渡する
- **transform** 動①変形[変化]する, 変える ②変換する
- **transport** 動輸送[運送]する 名輸送, 運送(機関)
- **transportation** 名交通(機関), 輸送手段
- **traveler** 名旅行者
- **traveling** 名旅行
- **treat** 動①扱う ②治療する ③おごる
- **treatment** 名①取り扱い, 待遇 ②治療(法)
- **treaty** 名条約, 協定 US-Japan Security Treaty 日米安全保障条約
- **Treaty of Paris** パリ条約《アメリカ合衆国とイギリスの間で結ばれた。イギリスがアメリカの独立を承認し, ミシシッピ川より東をアメリカ領とした, 1783》
- **tremendous** 形すさまじい, とても大きい
- **tremendously** 副恐ろしいほどに, 大いに
- **trend** 名トレンド, 傾向
- **trial** 名①試み, 試験 ②苦難 ③裁判 形試みの, 試験の
- **tribal** 形部族の, 同族的な
- **tribe** 名部族, 一族
- **tributary** 名(川の)支流
- **trigger** 名引き金, きっかけ, 要因
- **trillion** 名1兆
- **troop** 名隊
- **tropical** 形熱帯の
- **Tropicana Products** トロピカーナ・プロダクツ《社名》
- **troubled by** 《be –》～に悩まされている
- **troubling** 形厄介な
- **truck** 名トラック, 運搬車 pickup truck (後部荷台が無蓋の)小型トラック

America FAQ

- **trust** 動信用[信頼]する, 委託する 名信用, 信頼, 委託
- **trust territory** (国連による)信託統治地域
- **try out** 実際に試してみる
- **tuberculosis** 名結核
- **tune** 名①曲, 節 ②正しい調子[旋律]
- **turkey** 名七面鳥(の肉) roasted turkey 七面鳥の丸焼き
- **turn** in turn 順番に, 立ち代わって turn back 元に戻る turn to ～の方を向く turn up one's nose at ～を鼻であしらう
- **turning point** 転機, 岐路, ターニング・ポイント
- **typhoon** 名台風
- **typically** 副典型的に, いかにも～らしく
- **typify** 動典型となる, 特徴を表している, 類型化する
- **tyranny** 名専制政治, 暴政, 残虐

U

- **UN** 《U.N.とも》国際連合(=United Nations)
- **UN Charter** 国連憲章
- **UN Conference** 国連会議
- **UN PKO** 国連平和維持活動
- **unable** 形《be-to ～》～することができない
- **unalienable** 形譲渡できない, 不可譲の
- **uncertainty** 名不確かさ, 不安
- **uncomfortable** 形心地よくない
- **uncultivated** 形未開の
- **undaunted** 形ひるまない
- **undergo** 動経験する, 被る, 耐える
- **underground** 名地下
- **underlie** 動基礎となる, 下に横たわる
- **underlying** 形基本的な, 根本的な
- **underneath** 前～の下に, ～真下に 副下に[を], 根底は 名《the-》底部
- **underpin** 動(下から)支える, 裏打ちする
- **underwent** 動 undergo (経験する)の過去
- **undoubtedly** 副疑う余地なく
- **unemployed** 形雇われていない, 無職の, 失業中の
- **unemployment** 名失業(状態)
- **unfair** 形不公平な, 不当な
- **unfamiliar** 形よく知らない, なじみのない, 不案内な
- **unfortunately** 副不幸にも, 運悪く
- **unified** 形統一された, 統合された
- **unilateral** 形一方的な, 片側だけの
- **unimportant** 形重要でない, さいな, とるに足らない
- **uninterested** 形無関心な
- **union** 名①結合, 合併, 融合 ②連合国家
- **unique** 形唯一の, ユニークな, 独自の
- **uniquely** 副比類なく, 他に類を見ないほど
- **United Nations** 名《the-》国際連合(= U.N./UN)
- **unjust** 形不公平な, 不当な
- **unlawful** 形非合法的な, 違法の
- **unlikely** 形ありそうもない, 考えられない
- **unmarked** 形印[標示]のない
- **unresolved** 形解決していない

Word List

- **unrestrained** 形 抑制のない
- **unrestricted** 形 無制限の
- **unusual** 形 普通でない, 珍しい, 見[聞き]慣れない
- **unwelcome** 形 歓迎されない, 快く受け入れられない
- **up to** ①《be –》~する力がある, ~しようとしている, ~の責任[義務]である ②~まで, ~に至るまで, ~に匹敵して
- **upheaval** 名 大混乱[変動], 激変
- **upheld** 動 uphold（支持する）の過去, 過去分詞
- **uphill** 形 上りの, 坂を上って
- **upon** 前 ①《場所・接触》~（の上）に ②《日・時》~に ③《関係・従事》~に関して, ~について, ~して 副 前へ, 続けて
- **upper-middle class** 中流の上の階級の
- **upset** 形 憤慨して, 動揺して 動 気を悪くさせる, (心・神経など)をかき乱す
- **urban** 形 都会の, 都市の **urban decay** 都市の衰退
- **urbane** 形 都会風の, 洗練された
- **urge** 動 ①せき立てる, 強力に推し進める, かりたてる ②《- … to ~》…に~するよう熱心に勧める
- **US Census Bureau** 米国勢調査局
- **US-Japan Security Treaty** 日米安全保障条約
- **USA** 《U.S.A.とも》アメリカ合衆国（=United States of America）
- **use** 熟 **in use** 使用されて
- **used** 動 ①use（使う）の過去, 過去分詞 ②《- to》よく~したものだ, 以前は~であった 形 ①慣れている, 《get [become] – to》~に慣れてくる ②使われた, 中古の
- **user** 名 使用者, 利用者, 消費者
- **Utah** 名 ユタ州

V

- **vague** 形 漠然とした, あいまいな, かすかな
- **vain** 形 ①無益の, むだな ②うぬぼれが強い
- **valley** 名 谷, 谷間 **Death Valley** デスヴァレー《カリフォルニア州》
- **value** 名 価値, 値打ち, 価格 動 評価する, 値をつける, 大切にする
- **variety** 名 ①変化, 多様性, 寄せ集め ②種類
- **various** 形 変化に富んだ, さまざまの, たくさんの
- **vary** 動 変わる, 変える, 変更する, 異なる
- **vast** 形 広大な, 巨大な, ばく大な
- **vastness** 名 広大さ
- **Vatican** 名 ローマ法王(庁)
- **vehicle** 名 乗り物, 車, 車両
- **venture business** 冒険的事業
- **verdict** 名 判断, 意見
- **Vermont** 名 バーモント州
- **vessel** 名 ①(大型の)船 ②器, 容器 ③管, 脈管
- **vest** 名 ベスト, チョッキ
- **veteran** 名 ①ベテラン, 経験豊富な人 ②退役軍人, 老兵
- **veto** 名 拒否(権) 動 拒否する, 拒否権を行使する
- **via** 前 ~経由で, ~によって
- **viable** 形 実行可能な, 存続能力のある
- **vibrant** 形 響き渡る, 活気のある, (色が)鮮やかな
- **vicious** 形 悪意のある, 意地の悪い, 扱いにくい
- **victim** 名 犠牲者, 被害者
- **victory** 名 勝利, 優勝
- **video chat** ビデオチャット
- **Vietnam** 名 ベトナム《国名》

America FAQ

- **Vietnam War** ベトナム戦争《ベトナムの南北統一を巡って起こった戦争, 1960-1975》
- **Vietnamese** 名 ベトナム人
- **view** 熟 point of view 考え方, 視点
- **viewpoint** 名 見地, 観点, 見解
- **violate** 動 (法など)破る, 違反する
- **violation** 名 違反(行為), 侵害
- **violence** 名 ①暴力, 乱暴 ②激しさ
- **violent** 形 暴力的な, 激しい
- **violently** 副 激しく, 猛烈に, 暴力的に
- **Virgin Islands** バージン諸島
- **Virginia** 名 バージニア州
- **virtue** 名 ①徳, 高潔 ②美点, 長所 ③効力, 効き目
- **vision** 名 ①視力 ②先見, 洞察力
- **visiting music professor** 客員音楽教授
- **vocalization** 名 発声
- **vogue** 名 流行(品)
- **volume** 名 ①本, 巻, 冊 ②《-s》たくさん, 多量 ③量, 容積
- **voluntary** 形 自発的な, ボランティアの
- **volunteer** 名 志願者, ボランティア
- **volunteering** 名 ボランティアをすること
- **vote** 名 投票(権), 票決 votes cast 投票総数 動 投票する, 投票して決める
- **voter** 名 投票者
- **voyage** 名 航海, 航行, 空の旅

W

- **wage** 名 賃金, 給料, 応酬 wage differential 賃金格差
- **wagon** 名 荷馬車, ワゴン(車)
- **walk on** 歩き続ける
- **Wall Street** ウォール街《ニューヨークの金融街》
- **Walt Disney** ウォルト・ディズニー《アメリカのアニメーター, 映画監督, 実業家, 1901-1966》
- **war** civil war 内戦, 内乱 Civil War 南北戦争《1861-1865》 Cold War 冷戦 French and Indian Wars フレンチ・インディアン戦争《北アメリカ植民地で行われたフランス・インディアンの連合軍とイギリスとの戦争, 1755-1763》 Japanese-Russo War 日露戦争《日本とロシアの戦争, 1904-05》 Mexican War メキシコ戦争(メキシコ・アメリカ戦争)《1846-48》 Napoleonic Wars ナポレオン戦争《1799年から1815年まで続いた, ナポレオン率いるフランスとイギリスの抗争を軸にした諸戦争の総称》 post-Vietnam War ベトナム戦争後 Vietnam War ベトナム戦争《ベトナムの南北統一を巡って起こった戦争, 1960-1975》
- **War of Independence** 独立戦争
- **War on Terror** テロへの戦い
- **warming** 名 温度上昇, 暖まること
- **Warsaw** 名 ワルシャワ
- **warship** 名 軍艦
- **Washington, D.C.** ワシントンD.C.
- **WASP** 略 ワスプ《アングルサクソン系白人プロテスタントおよびそれによって構成される階層》
- **watering place** 給水場所
- **wave** 名 ①波 ②(手などを)振ること
- **way** 熟 all the way ずっと, はるばる, いろいろと along the way 途中で, これまでに, この先 go all the way ずっと, 完全に, 行くところま

Word List

で行く **in this way** このようにして **on the way** 途中で **this way** このように

- **wealth** 名 ①富, 財産 ②豊富, 多量
- **weapon** 名 武器, 兵器
- **weaponry** 名 《集合的に》兵器
- **wedding hall** 結婚式の会場
- **welcoming** 形 歓迎する
- **welfare** 名 ①福祉 ②福祉手当［事業］, 失業手当
- **well** 副 **as well** なお, その上, 同様に **as well as** ～と同様に **be well-ed** よく[十分に]～された
- **well-regulated** 形 よく整った
- **West Coast** ウェストコースト, 米国の西海岸
- **West Indies** 《the –》西インド諸島
- **West Palm Beach** ウェストパームビーチ《地名》
- **West Side Story** ウエスト・サイド物語《映画, 1961》
- **westerly** 形 西の, 西方への 副 西へ, 西から
- **western** 形 ①西の, 西側の ②《W-》西洋の 名 《W-》西部劇, ウェスタン
- **westward** 名 西方 形 西へ, 西向きの
- **whale** 名 クジラ(鯨)
- **whaling** 名 捕鯨
- **what ... for** どんな目的で
- **wheat** 名 小麦
- **whenever** 接 ①～するときはいつでも, ～するたびに ②いつ～しても
- **whereas** 接 ～であるのに対して[反して], ～である一方
- **whether** 接 ～かどうか, ～かまたは…, ～であろうとなかろうと **whether or not** ～かどうか
- **which** 熟 **of which** ～の中で
- **while** 熟 **for a while** しばらくの間, 少しの間
- **White Anglo-Saxon Protestant** ワスプ《アングルサクソン系白人プロテスタントおよびそれによって構成される階層》
- **Whitney** 《Mt. –》ホイットニー山
- **Whitney Museum** ホイットニー美術館
- **who** 熟 **those who** ～する人々
- **whole** 形 全体の, すべての, 完全な, 満～, 丸～ 名 《the –》全体, 全部
- **whom** 代 ①誰を[に] ②《関係代名詞》～するところの人, そしてその人を
- **wide** 形 幅の広い, 広範囲の, 幅が～ある 副 広く, 大きく開いて
- **widely** 副 広く, 広範囲にわたって
- **widescale** 形 広範囲の
- **widespread** 形 広範囲におよぶ, 広く知られた
- **wildcat bank** 山猫銀行《元は人里離れた銀行の意だったが, でたらめな営業を行うものが多かったため不良銀行の代名詞となった》
- **wilderness** 名 荒野, 荒れ地
- **wildlife** 名 野生生物
- **wing** 名 翼, 羽
- **Winston Churchill** ウィンストン・チャーチル《イギリスの政治家, イギリス戦時内閣の首相, 任期 1940-1945, 1951-1964(戦後)》
- **wipe** 動 ①～をふく, ぬぐう, ふきとる ②ぴしゃっと打つ
- **wire** 名 ①針金, 電線 ②電信
- **wisdom** 名 知恵, 賢明(さ)
- **withdrawn** 動 withdraw (引っ込める)の過去分詞 形 孤立した, 引きこもった
- **within** 前 ①～の中[内]に, ～の内部に ②～以内で, ～を越えないで

America FAQ

副中[内]へ[に], 内部に 名内部

- **witness** 名①証拠, 証言 ②目撃者 動①目撃する ②証言する
- **wonder** 動①不思議に思う, (〜に)驚く ②(〜かしらと)思う 名驚き(の念), 不思議なもの
- **work on** 〜で働く, 〜に取り組む, 〜を説得する, 〜に効く
- **work out** うまくいく, 何とかなる, (問題を)解く, 考え出す, 答えが出る, 〜の結果になる
- **workday** 名1日の労働時間
- **worker** 名仕事をする人, 労働者
- **working** 動 work (働く)の現在分詞 形働く, 作業の, 実用的な
- **workplace** 名職場, 仕事場
- **works of art** 芸術作品
- **world** 名 熟 all over the world 世界中に
- **World Series** ワールドシリーズ《野球》
- **World Trade Center** 世界貿易センター《2001年9月11日に起こった同時多発テロで崩壊》
- **World War II** 第二次世界大戦
- **world-wide** 形世界的な, 世界的規模の
- **worldwide** 形世界的な, 世界中に広がった, 世界規模の 副世界中に[で], 世界的に
- **worried** 動 worry (悩む)の過去, 過去分詞 形心配そうな, 不安げな **be worried about** (〜のことで)心配している, 〜が気になる[かかる]
- **worse** 形いっそう悪い, より劣った, よりひどい 副いっそう悪く
- **worsen** 動悪化する[させる]
- **worst** 形《the −》最も悪い, いちばんひどい 副最も悪く, いちばんひどく 名《the −》最悪の事態[人・物]
- **worth** 形(〜の)価値がある, (〜)しがいがある 名価値, 値打ち

- **wound** 名傷 動①負傷させる, (感情を)害する ②wind (巻く)の過去, 過去分詞
- **WWI** 略第一次世界大戦
- **WWII** 略第二次世界大戦
- **Wyoming** 名ワイオミング州

Y・Z

- **year-end** 形年末の
- **year-round** 形一年中の, 年間を通した
- **Yellowstone National Park** イエローストーン国立公園
- **yet** 熟 not yet まだ〜してない yet another さらにもう一つの
- **youngster** 名少年, 若者, 子ども
- **youth** 名若さ, 元気, 若者
- **zone** 名地帯, 区域 動区画[区分]する

E-CAT

English **C**onversational **A**bility **T**est
国際英語会話能力検定

● E-CATとは…
英語が話せるようになるための
テストです。インターネット
ベースで、30分であなたの発
話力をチェックします。

www.ecatexam.com

iTEP

● iTEP®とは…
世界各国の企業、政府機関、アメリカの大学
300校以上が、英語能力判定テストとして採用。
オンラインによる90分のテストで文法、リー
ディング、リスニング、ライティング、スピー
キングの5技能をスコア化。iTEP®は、留学、就
職、海外赴任などに必要な、世界に通用する英
語力を総合的に評価する画期的なテストです。

www.itepexamjapan.com

ラダーシリーズ
America FAQ アメリカ FAQ

2011年7月6日　第1刷発行
2021年2月5日　第6刷発行

著　者　西海 コエン

発行者　浦 晋亮

発行所　IBCパブリッシング株式会社
　　　　〒162-0804 東京都新宿区中里町29番3号
　　　　菱秀神楽坂ビル9F
　　　　Tel. 03-3513-4511　Fax. 03-3513-4512
　　　　www.ibcpub.co.jp

© IBC Publishing, Inc. 2011

印刷　**株式会社シナノパブリッシングプレス**
装丁　**伊藤 理恵**　　カバー写真　**photolibrary**
組版データ　Minion Pro Regular + Univers 67 Bold Condensed

落丁本・乱丁本は、小社宛にお送りください。送料小社負担にてお取り替えいたします。本書の無断複写（コピー）は著作権法上での例外を除き禁じられています。

Printed in Japan
ISBN978-4-7946-0089-9

本書は1997年に講談社インターナショナルから刊行された『アメリカQ&A』を増補・改訂したものです。

本書の情報は2011年初版発行時のものです。